CAMOUFLAGE
AT WAR

CAMOUFLAGE
AT WAR

AN ILLUSTRATED GUIDE FROM 1914 TO THE PRESENT DAY

MARTIN J. DOUGHERTY

CHARTWELL
BOOKS

Quarto is the authority on a wide range of topics.

Quarto educates, entertains and enriches the lives of our readers—enthusiasts and lovers of hands-on living.

www.quartoknows.com

This edition published in 2017 by
CHARTWELL BOOKS
an imprint of Book Sales
a division of Quarto Publishing Group USA Inc.
142 West 36th Street, 4th Floor
New York, New York 10018
USA

ISBN-13: 978-0-7858-3509-7

Project Editor: Michael Spilling
Design: Andrew Easton
Picture research: Terry Forshaw

10 9 8 7 6 5 4 3 2 1

Printed in China

Contents

INTRODUCTION

CONCEALMENT AND MISDIRECTION

Camouflage can grant strategic advantages or save a single life, but it can do neither if it is not properly understood and applied.

Camouflage can be defined as disguising military personnel and hardware by making them blend in with their surroundings. The intent is to conceal personnel, equipment and installations, but that is merely a means to an end. The underlying *purpose* of camouflage is to deceive the observer and thereby gain an advantage. It is of no real value in and of itself – hiding for hiding's sake does not achieve much.

Concealment and misdirection grant huge advantages to those who know how to make use of them. For this reason, camouflage training and the doctrine that governs its use must also cover how to make the most of the advantages offered by good camouflage. It is not enough to issue equipment without fostering an understanding of how best to use it; ideally,

Opposite: Generations of soldiers have concealed themselves by adding scraps of vegetation to their helmets and clothing. Effective camouflage makes use of both colour and shape.

the effective use of concealment and deception should be built into military training at all levels.

The infantryman needs to know how to remain concealed and to be confident in his ability to do so. He also needs to be aware of the enemy's camouflage capabilities and the limitations of his own. His commander needs to be able to provide him with a plan that makes best use of the infantryman's ability to remain concealed but that does not expect miracles from a bit of net and a few leafy branches. This continues all the way up the chain of command; officers need to be aware that what their reconnaissance assets see is not necessarily what is there – or not there – and to plan accordingly.

To be fully effective, then, camouflage measures must be implemented intelligently and with some purpose in mind. Lip service to the use of camouflage equipment might save a few lives, but the full potential of camouflage can only be realized by those who properly understand its capabilities and limitations.

Above: A US soldier uses a camouflage net somewhere in Iraq. The humble camouflage net has been a staple item of military equipment for around a century.

The concept of camouflage seems to be misunderstood in some quarters. This situation is not improved by elements of popular culture such as fashionable 'camouflage' clothing produced in bright colours, or supposedly realistic video games that allow players to add all manner of bizarre and highly visible 'camo' to their weapons.

Like many words adopted by popular culture, the term 'camouflage' seems to have been distorted almost beyond recognition. Perhaps as a result, most people seem to have a general idea of what camouflage is and what it does, but few have any idea how or why it works – or why it is so important.

Camouflage is one of several related activities that complement one another towards the end of deceiving the enemy. Which ones are used, and how effective they are, depends largely upon the nature of the deception being attempted. Typically, the aim is to deceive the enemy into thinking the camouflaged object is not there at all, or to cause them difficulty in attacking it with any accuracy. However, there are other possibilities, including creating a false target or influencing tactical decisions based on a misapprehension of the situation.

The use of camouflage can be simple and straightforward, or extremely elaborate. It can be a routine measure intended to provide some passive protection by making personnel and vehicles harder to spot and accurately attack, or part of a complex operation with a specific goal in mind.

Camouflage is an integral part of most modern military activity. Yet it was not always so, for the simple reason that concealment offered few advantages until the early 20th century. Before the invention of accurate long-range weapons, any advantage offered by concealment was outweighed by other factors. Military camouflage is thus quite a recent invention, and its development has been extremely rapid.

From Ostentation to Concealment

At very close range, there are few advantages to being hard to see. In ancient and early modern times, when the battlefield was dominated by hand weapons, bows and short-ranged muskets, concealment was of little use in an engagement. However, scouts might benefit from remaining undetected, and basic steps could be taken to reduce the detectability of a force. For example, armour might be dulled or covered to reduce the amount of sunlight glinting from metal. Such measures were useful in the approach to battle or during strategic movements, but as distance diminishes the chance of detection increases. In a face-to-face confrontation, other factors outweighed any advantage that might be had from concealment. Colourful jackets or helmet crests aided identification of friends and foes, while ostentation might intimidate an enemy.

The brightly coloured uniforms and tall hats of the Napoleonic era were important for morale on both sides. Uniforms helped build a sense of pride and identity, and clothing that made soldiers seem larger or more intimidating might weaken the enemy's resolve. There was no real

Below: An M113 Armoured Personnel Carrier pictured in 1984. Straight lines like those of the vehicle's blocky sides do not exist in nature. Foliage can help break up the outline.

Inspiration from the Zouaves

Many units raised for the American Civil War dressed as Zouaves, flamboyant North African troops in French service. Going to war in baggy, bright red trousers, a blue jacket and a fez may seem strange to modern observers, but it made perfect sense in the 1860s. However, the battlefield environment was changing.

Accurate long-ranged rifles enabled marksmen to pick a target and shoot at individuals. In the Civil War, officers adopted protective colouration by looking like any other soldier. Obvious trappings of rank, such as swords and revolvers, were carried at the back of the belt to be less obvious to enemy riflemen. Concealment was not the issue here, but not standing out as an attractive high-value target to sharpshooters was appreciated.

Right: Many variations on the Zouave costume existed, though the basic theme was much the same. Colourful, flamboyant dress contributed to a daredevil spirit and pride in the unit, which translated into military effectiveness.

ILLUST'D SWEET CAPORAL.
ZOUAVE, FRANCE, 1853.

consideration of camouflage or concealment; even the green uniforms adopted by rifle troops and some other light infantry were more a matter of tradition than concealment. Green was associated with hunters; it was due to this cultural association rather than a desire for concealment that green was often chosen for the uniforms of riflemen and sharpshooters. Any camouflage value that a green jacket had was largely coincidental.

In an era when an infantry engagement was typically decided by dense formations firing inaccurate weapons at one another at distances of 100 metres (328ft) or less, there was little to be gained by being hard to see and considerable benefit to be had from clothing that contributed to fighting spirit and regimental identity.

The British Army may have derived advantages from presenting a neat row of red jackets and white pith helmets in its battles against tribal enemies in Africa and India, but Boer riflemen were not intimidated and benefited from easily identified targets. Basic countermeasures included staining the white

Above: An island of red jackets lost in a sea of Zulus, this romanticised depiction of the battle of Isandlhwana in 1879 – where the British were comprehensively defeated – captures the spirit of the Colonial Era. The red jacket saw action for the last time just six years later.

helmet with coffee or otherwise darkening it, thereby reducing the visibility of infantry at a distance. By the end of the nineteenth century, British troops had relegated their red jackets to ceremonial occasions and adopted a dowdy khaki uniform that greatly reduced visibility.

US forces underwent a similar change from blue to khaki, along with a radical redesign of their uniforms, at the beginning of the 20th century. Not all nations followed suit; French uniforms, for example, were still their traditional blue. In any case, although these changes did reduce visibility at a distance they were only the most basic form of camouflage. Modern

techniques of disguising shape and colour were still many years off.

It is worth noting that many changes in army uniform were due to fashion rather than pragmatic reasons. In the mid-1800s, many nations favoured French-style uniforms, partly because they were very stylish but also because France was seen as one of the dominant military powers. Dressing like the French Army might help troops gain some of their panache and élan.

The uniforms of many nations changed after 1870. French-style blue jackets were replaced in some countries by grey. Although quite possibly less visible from a distance, these new uniforms were not adopted as camouflage but to be seen: the soldiers who wore them now looked more like Prussians, whose military efficiency had soundly defeated the French.

This trend continued, to a greater or lesser degree, to the present day. Although modern uniforms are designed with concealment in mind, there are other factors at play. Fashion is still important – even today, some changes follow those made by an influential nation rather than a need and benefit being clearly identified. Thus, not all changes in uniform represent progress towards perfect camouflage. Some are made to fit better in terms of appearance with an ally, or for reasons that may seem frivolous compared to giving soldiers better protection from observation and therefore the dangers of the battlefield.

Inspiration from Nature: Crypsis, Confusion and Colouration

In all forms of conflict there are advantages to not being seen, and to denying the opponent clear and accurate information. The most obvious example from nature is known as crypsis; colouration or other adaptations that assist a creature in remaining hidden.

Crypsis has advantages for both predators and prey. The prey animal may be able to hide and thus escape from the hunter or evade detection entirely. The predator can ambush its prey or creep closer before making its final dash, increasing the chance for success and reducing the energy expended in the attempt.

Concealment is only one aspect of this conflict between the need for information and attempts to deny it. Misdirection, confusion and deception are all useful tools for predator and prey alike. By seeming to be a harmless creature or object – a technique known as mimesis or mimicry – a predator may be overlooked by its prey. Conversely, by appearing to be a different species – perhaps a poisonous or highly dangerous one – a prey animal might deter aggression.

Some creatures are marked in ways that reduce the chance they will be recognized for what they are – a feature known as disruptive colouration. A variant on this concept is markings that make it difficult to distinguish features on a particular animal or to make out one individual in a herd.

Markings of this type can also increase the difficulty of estimating distance or how fast the animal is moving. This information is vital to a predator such as a cheetah, whose all-or-nothing sprint leaves little margin for error. If the predator cannot determine the likeliness of success, it may well wait for another opportunity.

Left: Crypsis in action: this Tanzanian caterpillar relies upon remaining unseen to protect itself from predators. Its resemblance to the tree bark is such that it would be all but invisible from even a short distance.

Many creatures use shape and the elimination of shadows. These are adapted to their environment in such a way that their outline tends to be lost amid the background, with telltale lines of shadow minimized when the animal is pressed close to a terrain feature such as a tree or rock.

The environment can be used to provide camouflage in other ways. Some creatures disguise themselves by attaching objects they have found, altering their appearance to the point where they may not be recognized. Others are adept at moving in such a way that they are lost against terrain features behind them.

A few creatures use complex methods of camouflage that involve altering their shape and/ or colouration to match the background or to seem like something the creature is not. Others are countershaded, giving them a different appearance when viewed from above and below, or have a gradual change in their colouration to

Above: The leopard uses its natural camouflage offensively rather than defensively. Its natural prey includes fleet-footed animals such as gazelle and impala. The ability to creep just one pace closer to prey before it flees can make the difference between a successful kill and starvation.

reduce the appearance of self-shadow and thus make the animal harder to distinguish.

Applying Nature's Principles to Human Conflict

The same principles apply in human conflict. Personnel, installations and hardware can be disguised, concealed or otherwise made hard to distinguish in order to gain the same advantages sought by predators and prey in the natural world. Since most combatants are both predators and prey, denying the enemy useful information is doubly important.

Camouflage and related measures serve the same purposes in war as in nature. They

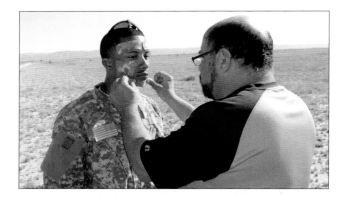

Left: New camouflage measures are constantly under development. Here, US personnel test a peel-and-stick facial concealment system at Fort Bliss Training Centre.

deny the opposition useful information about the size, shape and movement of an object or person, or even if it is there at all. This works mainly by tricking the eye – although it is also possible to conceal people or objects inside a larger structure. Although not camouflage as such, measures of this sort are often combined with some form of camouflage. If an object or person can be completely concealed, for example by remaining out of sight behind a wall or by lying down in a ditch or hole, then detection is not possible. However, this relies on the availability of suitable terrain features to offer concealment and can limit movement. This may be useful on a temporary basis or for elements that do not need to move around much, but those that have to manoeuvre need to be able to hide even where there is nothing to block the enemy's vision.

Hiding where an observer has a direct line of sight requires some measure of blending in with the background, which is best provided by well-applied camouflage. At the very least, the person or object hoping to remain concealed must not stand out: bright or glossy colours must be muted and movement

limited or conducted in a manner that will not attract attention. Altering shape can also be important; some shapes, such as straight lines, do not occur in nature and will stand out against a natural backdrop, although in an urban area straight-sided objects might be less noticeable than softer ones.

Fooling the Eye

The process by which the eye and brain create an impression of the local environment is complex, and can be fooled in many ways. The eye constantly scans and feeds information to the brain, which builds a model of the surrounding environment and updates it as new information comes in. Often this model is built with incomplete information,

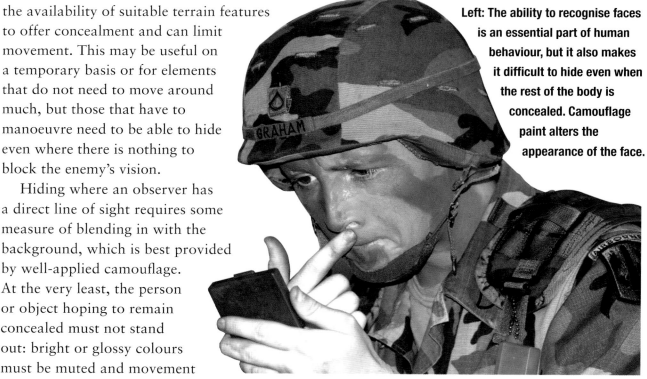

Left: The ability to recognise faces is an essential part of human behaviour, but it also makes it difficult to hide even when the rest of the body is concealed. Camouflage paint alters the appearance of the face.

with the brain filling in the gaps with a sort of predictive imagery based on what has been seen in the past.

This is why an object such as a strangely shaped tree stump can at first seem to be something different, but at second glance resolves into its true guise. The dog glimpsed from the corner of the eye is not really there; it is a construct made by the brain from incomplete visual data. When it draws attention, more data becomes available and an accurate image is created. Therefore, if attention is never drawn, the observer does not receive complete information on it. Effectively, the eye passes over the object and the brain ignores it.

The eye quickly recognizes familiar shapes such as human forms or objects it has seen many times. Disguising the general outline of an object can be enough to prevent this recognition taking place. Movement, or sometimes the lack of it,

Above: During the 1930s armoured warfare was in its infancy. These German Panzers have been concealed among haystacks as part of an exercise, demonstrating that even something as large and blocky as a tank can be effectively hidden.

will also draw the eye. A static object against a moving background will attract attention almost as readily as the opposite. The eye is also drawn to an object that is static and then begins to move, or one that stops moving. Thus, movement that fits with the general backdrop is far less likely to be observed.

Choosing Colours for Camouflage

Basic measures such as eliminating shiny polished metal and bright colours can reduce the likelihood of detection, but true camouflage goes much further. As well as altering the outline of a shape and muting its colours, camouflage

Above: Dressed in all white, Italian ski troops move through an Alpine landscape during World War I. Arctic and mountain terrain pose a unique problem for camouflaged troops, as the background can change colour rapidly due to altitude, season or weather conditions.

must blend in with the background. This means that camouflage designed to hide an object must use the same tones and shapes as the local environment. The closer the match, the better concealed the object will be.

Achieving this match can be difficult. Even a slight mismatch can stand out to a surprising degree, and not all colours are good camouflage. Black is generally too dark, even at night, and stands out a lot more than dark green or blue. In daylight, black can create a stark contrast with a natural background. Foliage colours may not work well in an urban environment where they do not occur so commonly. Light conditions and the brightness of colours are also critical. A piece of camouflaged material might be the

right colour but be too intense compared to the background and so will stand out.

The interplay of light, tone and brightness can be observed by watching a ginger cat move through undergrowth. In good light, a bright orange cat is very obvious among the surrounding greenery, but in twilight it can all but disappear. This is because colour is less important in poor light conditions than intensity; a lighter, darker or more intensely coloured patch can stand out more than an area that is the wrong colour but of an equivalent vividness.

Nature has few very vivid or pure colours, so using them in camouflage is inappropriate. A technical term for how vivid a colour appears is saturation. A pure colour is 100% saturated, with plain grey as the 0% mark.

Opposite: Coalition forces operating in Iraq and Afghanistan are under constant threat from attack. The only effective solution is to deploy protective sniper teams. A well-concealed sniper can eliminate any threat.

Dazzle Colour Schemes

One form of information denial does not attempt to conceal the object, but makes it difficult to obtain good information about it. Just as it can be hard to see where one zebra in a herd ends and another begins, objects can be made difficult to resolve. One example of this was the use of 'dazzle' colour schemes to protect ships during the two World Wars.

Although the zebra-stripe pattern of dazzle camouflage probably made the ships more obvious, it also made it difficult to determine their direction or speed from a distance. Since torpedo and gun firing solutions required this data, the attacker's task became far more difficult. Dazzle may have deterred many attacks; with a limited stock of torpedoes, submarines would only expend them with a good chance of a hit. If confidence in the firing solution was low, the attack might be called off.

Estimating the speed and heading of a ship is made vastly more difficult by dazzle paint schemes that draw the eye away from key features of a ship and create the impression of a different shape.

Most camouflage materials use colours that are not highly saturated – although saturation, like everything else, must be matched to the background.

The effectiveness of camouflage depends on distance and the conditions the observer is experiencing. At long distances, light blue or grey can be hard to distinguish even though these colours are very obvious up close. Distance also puts more clutter in the observer's field of view and increases the chance that the observer's eye will be distracted by some more obvious object.

The Military Value of Camouflage

Even the very best conventional camouflage does not grant invisibility; it reduces the distance at which the camouflaged object is likely to be detected and increases the time before it can be clearly identified. This is useful when the observer has only a fleeting opportunity to build a picture of the situation.

A ground-attack pilot hurtling at great speed has only a few seconds to identify the target and set up an attack; soldiers responding to an ambush must quickly locate the source of enemy fire while under great stress. Targets or ambushers that stand out are likely to be engaged; those using even the most rudimentary camouflage may not be.

Camouflage, then, is all about playing the odds. There are no guarantees, but good camouflage stacks the deck against the observer. This can be useful for defensive purposes, reducing the chances of a successful enemy attack, or offensive ones, by allowing an ambush or concealed approach. Camouflage can also

be used to deny the enemy information about something he knows is there.

For example, the enemy might have detected the presence of an armoured force, but camouflage makes it difficult to determine how many vehicles there are and their precise nature. It may not even be possible to discover whether the vehicles are real or decoys.

Deception and Decoys

Deception using decoys and other methods is a separate field, but one closely tied to the use of camouflage. No decoy is completely lifelike; in most cases it should not be hard to tell a real target from a fake from a modest distance. However, if the real target is concealed or camouflaged, it might not even be noticed.

Below: British soldiers take part in a live fire exercise somewhere in the Saudi Arabian desert, January 1991. They are wearing a two-tone, desert version of the British Army's Disruptive Pattern Material (DPM) camouflage. DPM was introduced in the 1960s and remained in service until a new pattern was introduced in 2010.

An enemy expecting to see a tank or bunker and presented with something that looks like one may accept it as real without question, distracting his fire from the real target.

Creating decoys and dummies good enough to momentarily fool an attack pilot or an enemy tank gunner is one thing. Creating a false image that can convince enemy scouts and intelligence analysts is much harder. Here, too, camouflage has an important part to play. If little attempt is made to conceal real targets, then decoys are unlikely to work. However, if it is already difficult to determine if that vaguely glimpsed shape really is a tank then the decoy has a greater chance of succeeding.

In this situation, camouflage effectively reduces the level of certainty the enemy can have about any given object. Rather than spotting what are obviously tanks, an observer must infer from vague impressions that tanks are present. This lowers the quality of data that will be accepted as true, and makes it more likely that some other objects that give the impression of being tanks might be accepted as real.

Camouflage is, of course, useless if the target advertises its presence and location in some manner. Until the invention of electronic sensors, noise was the most likely giveaway and the only means of detection was human senses. If audible noise and perhaps any telltale smell were kept to a minimum, and camouflage was likely to defeat the observer's eye, then the target was probably safe. That situation has changed dramatically in recent years.

Fooling Thermal Sensors

Most camouflage methods are optical: they are designed to fool the human eye, which can detect only a limited range of wavelengths. Modern electronic sensors can 'see' a much wider segment of the electromagnetic spectrum and can render conventional camouflage useless. Thermal, or infrared, sensors operate outside the visual spectrum, and can 'see' the heat emissions from a target. Thermal sensors are passive: they detect emissions rather than emitting any signal themselves. All objects that are at a temperature above Absolute Zero (−273° Celsius, and not possible anywhere on Earth) have some thermal emissions and can in theory be detected by this means.

However, thermal sensors cannot distinguish between objects that are at exactly the same temperature or very close to it. A vehicle that has been standing for several hours and is at the same temperature as the building behind it cannot be detected; all that can be seen is a large expanse that is emitting the same amount of heat. If the vehicle were at a lower or higher temperature than the building, it would be visible providing the thermal sensor had sufficiently good resolution.

Hiding an object from thermal sensors requires somehow maintaining it at the same temperature as its surroundings – which is probably not possible – or else concealing its thermal signature. This usually requires placing a physical barrier between the sensor and the emission. This could be achieved by exploiting terrain, as thermal sensors cannot see through a hillside or thick foliage.

Alternatively, thermal signature can be disguised in various ways. A vehicle with camouflage netting draped directly over it will probably be recognizable; however, one that has netting or foliage around it partially blocking the view of the sensor might not be so obvious, as its outline will be broken up by the

Opposite: In recent years, thermal and low-light detection systems have become widely available on the open market. They do not render camouflage obsolete, but they do add a new dimension to the problem of concealment.

lower-temperature obstructions. It will still be apparent that something is there, but exactly what it is may be unclear.

Concealing Emissions

Detection of other emissions can render camouflage useless as well. Active emissions are any signals – in any part of the electromagnetic spectrum – sent out by the target. This can be something as simple as putting a vehicle's lights on. Headlights are an active emission in the visual spectrum and can, of course, be spotted by the human eye. Sound, such as the noise of an engine, is another active emission that can

betray the existence and position of a target. Visual camouflage is far less useful once the installation or vehicle has attracted attention, even if it then stops producing noise and light.

Radio transmissions, and the emissions of various sensors, can also be detected. If a vehicle or installation reveals its existence by transmitting when the enemy is trying to detect radio signals, it provokes interest, which may lead to discovery even if the enemy cannot pinpoint its exact location by radio direction finding. Emissions of this sort can be reduced in various ways such as keeping transmissions short and of relatively low power.

Radar can be used to detect objects such as vehicles, aircraft and buildings even if they cannot be seen through some visually opaque medium such as clouds, mist or camouflage netting. Radar relies on the active emission of a signal and the detection of its return: the radar system emits a pulse and analyses what bounces back. Angular, metallic objects reflect more strongly than softer, natural structures, and traditional camouflage paint or netting is of no use in defeating radar. Concealment can be achieved by placing a barrier in the way – radar cannot see through hills or walls – or by reducing the amount of radar energy reflected.

Acoustic methods can be used in a similar manner underwater. A pulse of sound energy sent out by a sonar system will be reflected and scattered by every object it encounters, enabling a receiver to build up a picture of the surroundings. A measure of concealment is possible by reducing the amount of sound energy reflected by a vessel.

Of course, both sonar and radar used in this manner are active systems; that is, they emit pulses that can be detected by others. The effect is like two people looking for one another in the dark, one of whom uses a flashlight. The light might well find the target, but it can be detected from a greater distance than is useful. The decision to use active systems reduces the usefulness of any camouflage that is in use but may be necessary to carrying out a mission. Thus there are methods to make active emissions less detectable; a sort of camouflage applied to electromagnetic signals.

The addition of this electromagnetic dimension to the military environment has created the need to think in terms of a 'four-dimensional battlespace' (where the fourth dimension is the electromagnetic spectrum) rather than in three dimensions with reference only to what can be seen by eye.

However, the concept of camouflage has not changed, and countermeasures have been created to match the capabilities of new sensors. The conflict between information gathering and information denial continues unabated, and camouflage techniques are keeping pace.

CHAPTER 1

INFANTRY CAMOUFLAGE IN THE WORLD WARS

Rapid changes in warfare took place in the nineteenth century, making brightly coloured uniforms a liability and greatly increasing the importance of concealment on the battlefield.

The principles of camouflage and concealment were well known before the beginning of the twentieth century. Hunters sometimes concealed themselves using a stalking horse; a mobile screen behind which they could remain unobserved while approaching the quarry. And, although the adoption of green uniforms for sharpshooters and rifle troops was based on fashion rather than pragmatism, it did grant some concealment compared to the brighter and less natural colours worn by line regiments.

There are references to the use of camouflage dating back many centuries. In Shakespeare's play *Macbeth*, Malcolm's army uses branches from Birnam Wood to conceal its advance. This

Opposite: Dressed in a World War II SS uniform, this modern re-enactor wears a face veil to obscure any glare. He wears a 'plane tree' pattern SS camouflage smock and has garnished his helmet with some straw. This outfit was probably worn by a sniper during the Normandy campaign of June–July 1944.

stratagem might have sprung purely from the playwright's imagination, but the idea of making a force less obvious by carrying branches is not without merit. At a distance, the outlines of men would be altered by the foliage they carried and might blend into the background. How well this might have worked when the army was on the march is open to some debate.

Camouflage was, however, of relatively little use in an era of large, densely packed formations. Not only were the men and horses themselves rather obvious, but they would often kick up a great deal of dust as they marched, making it unlikely that individual camouflage would have any effect. This dust was in part the inspiration for the very first uniform intended to reduce visibility.

The Invention of Khaki

In 1846, the Corps of Guides was raised by the British Indian Army for service on the Northwest Frontier, where conditions were described as resembling a sea of dust. Initially the corps was small, although it consisted of both infantry and foot elements, and personnel dressed in the traditional clothing of the region.

In 1848, it was decided to create a uniform for the Corps of Guides, and rather than the red jackets of other regiments they were given clothing of a drab light brown colour intended to match the sea of dust they operated in. This was done with the explicit intent that the Guides would be lost to sight in it. The colour of this new uniform was named 'khaki', from a Hindi word meaning 'soil-coloured' but often loosely translated as 'dirt'.

Below: Most British infantry in the Napoleonic era wore the distinctive red coat, a colour originally chosen mainly for the availability of dye that would not run in wet conditions. The newly raised 95th Rifles (left) had their origins in an experimental rifle corps and instead wore green, reflecting the association between rifle troops and hunters.

This was not a camouflage uniform in the modern sense, as it made no attempt to break up the soldier's outline and was of a single colour. It was, however, the first real move in that direction and might be considered the beginning of modern camouflage uniforms. Had the Corps of Guides been less effective, the idea might have been ignored and forgotten. However, the corps proved highly useful and was greatly expanded over time. Meanwhile, khaki was adopted by other regiments of the British Indian Army.

The Spread of Field Colours

Sir Robert Napier's expedition to Abyssinia (1867–68), an expensive but extremely successful operation to rescue hostages taken by King Theodore II, employed troops from India dressed in khaki, and by the 1880s khaki was standard for colonial campaigns. Despite, this, some of the British troops deployed to the Sudan to fight the Mahdist rebellion wore their red tunics in action.

The final occasion where British forces fought in red rather than khaki was at Gennis in the Sudan, in December 1885. Khaki was standardized throughout the British Army in 1902, with the adoption of the new service dress. This was the uniform in which the British Army went to war in 1914.

Meanwhile, a similar change occurred in the uniforms of the United States military. Modifications in 1881 included a dress helmet with a spike – not unlike that of the Prussian army, which was at that time regarded as the finest in Continental Europe. This was short-lived, and during the 1880s the US Army lost its traditional blue uniforms for a more pragmatic design in khaki. By the outbreak of the Spanish-American War of 1898, the army had adopted a khaki field service uniform, although this was not available in time for the conflict.

Above: At the 1897 Battle of Dargai (in modern Pakistan) British troops wore khaki, but vestiges of the 'old ways' still existed. The gallantry of wounded piper George Findlater, playing the troops forward despite being exposed to enemy fire, perhaps belonged to an earlier era.

Evolution continued until 1902, when regulations standardized the new khaki uniform. Implementation was slow, however, and as late as 1911 some units of the US army were being issued uniform from old stocks. New variations continued to appear, but by 1911 the US Army had achieved its distinctive early 20th century appearance and was dressed in khaki or olive drab for the field.

In Continental Europe, France clung to its traditional predominantly blue uniforms, while Prussia led the unification of the German states and Germany emerged as a new world power.

German troops at first wore the traditional *Waffenrock* (uniform) of the Prussian army. This was dark blue for infantry and artillery and light blue for most cavalry. Light infantry (*Jaeger*) units wore dark green.

The German army adopted *feldgrau* (field grey, a greenish-grey) uniforms for field service in 1907–10, retaining the Waffenrock for use when not in the field. This new Feldrock (field uniform) was later simplified but retained its general character. *Feldgrau* was lighter in hue than the khaki used by many other nations, but offered similar low-visibility advantages. Light grey clothing had long been known to blend into the horizon at distances of 150 metres (490ft), making grey a good choice for field service.

Russian troops of the same era wore dark green tunics and trousers, with a dark green or grey overcoat in winter. White jackets were used

in the summer, although these may have been dyed khaki for field service. Thus the armies of the great powers were mostly dressed in dowdy green and grey by the outbreak of the Great War. The most notable exception was the French army.

Infantry Camouflage in the Great War

At the outbreak of World War I, military technology was developing fast and had been for some time. With hindsight it is easy to see that all the critical lessons were there, and that the tactics and doctrine of the time should have been revised to account for the new weaponry capabilities. However, there were good reasons to suppose that any new war in Europe would be won in the traditional manner: by rapid movement of forces to outmanoeuvre one another, followed by a combination of firepower and shock action.

Above: French troops pose for the camera dressed in their traditional bright red trousers and sky-blue tunics. The early exchanges of the Great War quickly demonstrated the high visibility of such a colour scheme.

At the outbreak of the Great War, it was expected that aggression, élan and offensive spirit could win battles as they had during the Austro–Prussian war of 1866 or the Franco–Prussian war of 1870. This was not unreasonable, especially since experience of conflict after that date tended to come from colonial 'small wars', which did not prepare the armies of Europe to fight one another on a grand scale.

The opening weeks of the Great War did, in fact, unfold much as expected. Casualties were heavier than expected when attacking, but despite this the Central Powers managed to shove the British and French armies back and prevent them from establishing a defensive line. This was due in part to rapid manoeuvre, flanking forces that were attempting to establish a defensive position or driving off their supports to threaten an envelopment.

Cavalry played a part in this war of advance and manoeuvre, sometimes as mounted riflemen. Cavalry were able to close with the enemy and deliver shock action with sabre, revolver and lance, but opportunities were rare. The retreat from Mons in 1914 was the last occasion on which British artillery deployed wheel to wheel in the open in the Napoleonic fashion; after this, the nature of warfare changed considerably.

Forced into the Modern Age

The Great War rapidly stagnated into trench warfare, because the Western Allies managed to stave off complete rout by a fighting retreat and valiant counterattacks 'in the old style'. The French army of this era went into action looking not unlike it did in 1814 under Napoleon. As early as 1911, those who recognized that times were changing advocated the replacement of the traditional bright red trousers with something less obvious, but were rebuffed by the traditionalists. The Minister of War reportedly dismissed the idea on the grounds that 'France IS red trousers!'

Thus, while other armies were adopting a low-visibility uniform, the French retained their glamour. In the early weeks of the Great War, cavalry charged wearing shining steel breastplates and crested helmets; infantry columns advanced with bands playing at their head. This was the last hurrah of the old order, and it was as wasteful as it was magnificent. Yet the German advance was slowed and finally brought to a stop by these brightly dressed and highly motivated young soldiers.

Even before the outbreak of the Great War, it was suspected that the French infantryman

in his iron-blue coat and red trousers was simply too obvious and thus an easy target for an enemy force that now consisted entirely of sharpshooters and machinegunners. Now, with graphic proof in the form of enormous casualty figures, France began taking the idea of camouflage seriously. Indeed, the French gave us the term 'camouflage' and recruited a corps of camoufleurs to implement it.

Experiments with a more muted blue for the jacket proved problematic, not least since some of the chemicals used to make the chosen dyes were only available from enemy countries. Early attempts at a less visible jacket for the French infantryman resulted in a dye that quickly faded to light grey, but by late 1915 a more stable 'horizon blue' was in use. This proved much less visible than the previous colours, especially in poor light conditions. Recruits were often issued older uniforms from stocks, replacing them with horizon blue before deploying to the battlefront.

Cloth for the new uniforms was in limited supply, so initially it was used to produce greatcoats and hats, with trousers and other garments worn under the coat continuing to use brighter blue cloth until stocks were sufficient that all garments could be horizon blue. Another measure to get appropriate clothing to the troops was to use civilian jackets that were roughly the right colour, without being too particular about uniform regulations. Thus, some French troops wore green or brown jackets in the field.

Coping with Poor Visibility

The popular image of the Great War is that of two armies bombarding one another with artillery while huddling in trenches until tanks finally came along to break the deadlock. In such an environment, camouflage would seem to have little relevance. Similarly, those who believe

Infantry Uniforms in World War I

Although infantry uniforms evolved quickly during the Great War, the need to make troops less visible warred with the need to equip vast numbers of men, slowing implementation of life-saving refinements.

French Corporal (1915)
By 1915, French infantry were dressed in 'horizon blue', which blended into the hazy distance far better than the old uniform.

French Infantryman (1914)
In sky-blue tunic, the French infantryman of 1914 would not look out of place on a battlefield of half a century earlier.

German Cavalry Officer (1915)
Germany fielded large numbers of Uhlans (lancers) whose uniforms retained ornamental piping and the distinctive *czapka* helmet from another era.

German Colonial Infantry (1915)
Other theatres of war required their own low-visibility clothing, such as this German *Schutztruppen* uniform issued for service in East Africa.

British Infantryman (1916)
This British Army private is typical of those who fought on the Western Front, with a khaki tunic and Mk I steel helmet.

Russian Infantryman (1916)
The Russian army favoured an olive green uniform well suited to conditions in Eastern Europe and the Baltic.

German Mountain Trooper (1917)
The beginnings of World War II era uniforms can be seen in the colour and cut of this German mountain rifleman's grey-green clothing.

German Stormtrooper (1918)
This stormtrooper's field grey M1915 uniform is typical of the German soldier in 1918. The shiny buttons are covered with a fly front to avoid reflection.

Above: Late-war German 'stormtrooper' tactics were based around firepower, speed and aggression, but relied heavily upon concealment during both the approach and the actual assault.

that all attacks in the Great War were made by neat lines of soldiers herded onto the guns by their officers may wonder if concealment played any useful part.

In fact, this impression of the conflict is based on some things that did happen, but is a distorted picture of the war as a whole. Infantry attacks were often made as a series of moves from cover to cover, with small parties rather than whole battalions as the tactical elements. The targets offered to the enemy were thus relatively small, and although machine guns were present in very large numbers the majority of defenders were armed with bolt-action rifles that required accurate aim.

Visibility during an attack on the Western Front was never good. Weather conditions might

daylight attacks across no-man's land were only a small proportion of the activity on the front lines. Most of the time troops were essentially on a highly dangerous form of garrison duty where the main threat was from artillery fire. Both sides quickly learned that appearing above the parapet was dangerous.

Even with the use of periscopes for observation, it was not always possible to remain completely concealed within the trenches. Personnel had to raise their heads to shoot, and some sections of the trench would be under enemy observation and thus potentially under fire. If the enemy occupied high ground or constructed an elevated position, it became possible to shoot into some sections of the trenches. Similarly, some areas were too shallow to offer good protection.

These areas quickly became known to both sides, but it was not possible to avoid using them. Here again, reduced visibility was an advantage. Even if the soldier was spotted moving through a vulnerable section of trench, enemy riflemen had to make an accurate shot before he moved out of sight. Any reduction in visibility deprived the enemy of possible aim points and could make the difference between life and death.

Eastern Front

On the Eastern Front, and in other theatres such as Africa and Palestine, conditions were different. The war in the East never stagnated to the same degree as the Western Front. Trench warfare occurred, but the Eastern Front remained far more fluid than the war in the West. This created different opportunities for concealment and ambush, although the same general principles applied everywhere. Camouflage as such was not a day-to-day factor in military operations, but the value of being less

contribute with mist and rain, and the inevitable smoke of battle made visibility difficult. Riflemen shooting at even a fairly large block of troops at ranges of 200 metres (650ft) or more were likely to miss many of their shots. If the targets were actually small groups moving from cover to cover, wearing clothing that blended into the mud of the battlefield or the haze above it, accurate fire became very difficult.

The benefits of a less obvious uniform are readily apparent in this environment, but

Fighting at Night

Many operations, including raids on enemy trenches, wire cutting or repair, and repairs to local trenches, were undertaken at night. The uniforms worn by all combatant nations offered fairly good concealment at night, especially when precautions were taken to remove reflective objects and to reduce noise. Night-time did not bring safety, however. At any moment, the area might be illuminated by flares if one side or the other suspected activity between the trenches.

The light conditions thus created were not ideal, with flares flickering and creating shadows at strange angles. It was not uncommon for static objects such as wire posts to seem as if they were moving or to be misidentified, potentially drawing fire in the wrong places or where no threat existed. For personnel caught in the open when a flare went up, shape and movement were far more important than the colours they wore.

The best option was to get down and stay still until the light faded, although some of the concepts of camouflage were still applicable in this situation. Distinctive shapes like rifles and helmets were likely to give personnel away, and any glint of light from metal was to be avoided.

Those who learned to disguise shapes, including their own, were far more likely to survive. The best way to disguise shape was to become part of the ground clutter; here, once again, the uniforms of the Great War offered concealment that the previous generation of equipment had not.

Above: These Australian soldiers are pictured with a captured Turkish sniper. His 'garnish' of foliage does more than blend in with the local vegetation in terms of colour; it also breaks up and softens the distinctive outline of his body and rifle, removing points of contrast that would otherwise draw the eye.

visible was well appreciated and at least some efforts were made to improve this capability.

Camouflage, at least of a rudimentary sort, routinely saved lives even when troops were not engaged in an attack. It also made it possible to undertake covert observation and sniping. Both required a clear view of enemy positions, or at least part of them, and that meant vulnerability if the sniper or observer were spotted. Some of the measures taken to reduce this vulnerability are still part of modern sniping technique.

Snipers and Observers

The early twentieth century was the era of the bolt-action rifle. Machine guns were available, and proved effective in defence, but the rifle fire of individual soldiers dominated the battlefield.

Above: This papier-mâché hide makes use of the fact that dead horses were a frequent feature of the landscape. Horses were widely used for transportation on the Western Front, and became casualties in large numbers.

The days of massed volley fire were gone; soldiers were now taught to aim and shoot when a target presented itself, and marksmanship was highly prized.

However, the capability of soldiers to shoot accurately – and indeed, to pull the trigger on someone knowing he would likely die – varied considerably. As a result, both sides in the Great War began to field specialist sniper units. These were made up of men who were willing to pick a target and kill him, and to do so accurately, but who were also excellent observers and skilled at concealment.

The first specialist sniping units were probably fielded by the German Army, but other nations soon followed suit. The first British force recognized as specialist snipers was formed from the Lovat Scouts, a Highland regiment, which contained a significant number of men who had previously been gamekeepers. These men, colloquially known as Ghillies, were excellent riflemen who understood how to stalk prey and to remain concealed.

Renamed the Lovat Scouts Sharpshooters, the new sniper unit proved highly effective and, more importantly, survivable. This was partly due to an understanding of what the prey, or enemy, could see and what he could not and partly to discretion about when to shoot and when to remain hidden. A key tool was what became known as the Ghillie suit, which is nowadays associated with snipers but at the time was only used by gamekeepers.

Methods used by snipers included creeping out into no-man's land at night and remaining hidden there all day before returning, or the apparently safer option of finding an elevated spot behind friendly lines. Another option was the creation of armoured loopholes in the trench parapet, allowing a rifleman to shoot in relative safety.

The Ghillie Suit

The Ghillie suit consisted of a base garment, usually tan, painted in irregular and natural-looking browns and greens. There was no 'pattern' as such; the aim was to avoid symmetry and anything that seemed too regular to blend in with nature. The coat was matched with a hood, facemask and gloves in similar colours.

The former Ghillies of the Lovat Scouts Sharpshooters based their designs on what they knew would work against wary prey animals such as deer. They already possessed an eye for local conditions and adapted their designs accordingly. Combined with an ability to select a good position and the patience to remain still for long periods, their unique equipment enabled them to be highly effective and encouraged the expansion of the sniper programme.

Right: The Ghillie suit was introduced by the Lovat Scouts during the Great War, and variants of the concept became common equipment for snipers. This photo, taken in 1941, illustrates both the use of the suit and netting. Even without 'garnish' the net considerably softens the outline of the wearer.

Above: Infantry camouflage remained in its infancy during World War I. By World War II, specialists – such as this re-enactor dressed as a German sniper – were creating their own camouflage dress, including face masks and webbing to obscure the reflection of a rifle's metal parts.

Concealment was the sniper's best defence, since a number of countermeasures existed. Counter-sniper fire was an option, or the fire of several less skilled riflemen. A volley of grenades or mortar bombs might be sent the way of a suspected sniper, and in some cases the supporting artillery might be willing to lend a hand. Armoured loopholes were sometimes countered by the use of powerful weapons – at least one unit obtained an elephant gun for the purpose.

Rifle fire from the other side of no-man's land was a constant threat to troops in the trenches, but snipers were particularly hated because their shots were more personal – and more likely to be lethal. A live-and-let-live attitude often prevailed in the trenches, with troops shooting in self-defence but not making great efforts to harm the enemy if it did not seem necessary. Snipers tended to be far more motivated, and also persistent. Since the presence of a suspected sniper might bring down artillery fire or at least increased enemy activity, even friendly snipers tended to be resented as making a horrible experience still worse for everyone.

Snipers' Devices

Despite this, snipers went about their business on both sides, often using highly inventive methods. One such was the creation of fake trees. No-man's land contained a great many tree stumps or blasted trunks, which both sides were used to seeing. After photographing a suitable tree and constructing an artificial version that looked sufficiently like it, a risky construction operation was undertaken at night to replace it with the fake – which contained an observation or sniper post.

Above: Having joined the Great War later than their European allies, American troops were behind the learning curve regarding camouflage technique. Here, British personnel instruct American snipers in current techniques, with particular emphasis on disguising the shape of the head and shoulders.

To the enemy, it appeared that nothing had changed, but now an observer or sniper had a position in no-man's land that the enemy was used to ignoring as harmless. The amount of effort required to set up such a position was considerable, but knowledge of the enemy's activities could be worth much more. Sniping from such a position would inevitably lead to its discovery sooner or later, which made the choice of how best to use it a difficult one.

This choice exists in all uses of a camouflaged or concealed position. The value of use must be balanced against the risk or consequences of detection. 'Routine' sniping, i.e. harassing the enemy by shooting targets of opportunity, did not produce sufficiently valuable results to be worth revealing an elaborately constructed position. However, a high-value target such as a visiting senior officer might justify the risk.

Similarly, using the same position repeatedly might result in the enemy watching it and either using countersniping or just plastering it with artillery from time to time. Concealment was no defence against speculative fire, and the chances of successfully remaining concealed decreased once the enemy realized a particular position was being used.

Thayer and Dazzle Camouflage

Thayer was convinced that all animals were camouflaged, mostly by the use of countershading. Although this viewpoint has been widely challenged, Thayer's work remains highly influential. He was the source of the term 'dazzle' applied to camouflage intended to confuse the viewer, although he called it 'razzle dazzle'. He also proposed to the British Army that camouflage-patterned field uniforms should be adopted. This idea was years ahead of its time and was not implemented. Brush's work diverged from that of Thayer in some areas. Working with his artist wife Mary, he tried to find ways to camouflage aircraft, including an attempt to create a mostly transparent aircraft.

In largely static conditions such as the Western Front, the number of useful sniping and observation points just behind the line was very limited, so for the enemy it eventually became a question of whether a given spot was currently in use rather than wondering where an observer or sniper might be. This made concealment ever more important, since remaining hidden when the enemy knew where to look was even more of a challenge.

The Pioneering Camoufleurs

The first corps of 'camoufleurs' was formed by the French during the Great War. There were at the time no camouflage experts as such, so camoufleurs were recruited from those with relevant experience of concealment in the natural world or of using colour and shade to obtain a desired effect. This collection of painters and naturalists was augmented by experts in psychology and designed much of the camouflage of the era. Their work still forms the basis of modern camouflage theory.

Many of the painters-turned-camoufluers were influenced by or members of the Impressionist school, and were adept at creating the impression of an object or scene with a few shapes. Others were Cubists whose angular shapes could be used to confuse the eye or create a false image. Observation of how animals used colouration to conceal themselves informed much of the camoufleurs' work, with many ideas drawn from the book *Concealing Coloration in the Animal Kingdom* by Abbott Henderson Thayer (1909).

Thayer's name is widely connected with the study of military concealment, and he is sometimes referred to as the Father of Camouflage. This is a little misleading, as his primary contribution was a study of the principles on which camouflage came to be based, which was then put to practical use by others.

However, Thayer was involved in some practical camouflage work. In 1898 he and a colleague, George de Forest Brush, began work on a way to conceal warships using countershading. In 1902 they obtained a patent for their method, which used changes in colouration to alter the appearance of an object. At its most basic, the idea was to darken the areas most brightly lit and lighten those that would normally be in shadow. The effect was to make the shape of the object difficult to discern by depriving the viewer of clearly defined shapes and areas of shadow.

Left: The use of fake trees was an ingenious method of creating an observation post. The enemy would probably notice a tree that was not there previously, so an existing trunk had to be replaced with a convincing copy – which was then set up in a rather hazardous overnight removal and construction project.

In Britain, the idea of using countershading and disruptive patterning to protect naval vessels was first proposed by John Graham Kerr in 1914. The idea found favour with Winston Churchill, then First Lord of the Admiralty. Kerr was not seeking to conceal ships but to make it as difficult as possible to distinguish their features. Countershading would hide the shape of guns, while disruptive patches of white would hide the ship's general outline.

Implementation of Kerr's idea was haphazard and patchy, and after Churchill was replaced as First Lord of the Admiralty the idea of camouflaging ships was temporarily abandoned. It was revived by Norman Wilkinson, who implemented a programme of what became known as dazzle camouflage. He was credited with inventing it, an assertion challenged in court by Kerr but eventually upheld. During the legal scuffling, Wilkinson maintained that Kerr's aim had been to completely hide ships rather than his (and Wilkinson's) intention of making them harder for enemy gunners to hit.

Further Developments

The concept of the Ghillie suit was well proven in the Great War, although it was known by other names in some regions. One alternative term is 'Yowie' suit. This term was probably coined by Australian troops due to the suit's resemblance to the mythical Yowie, an Australian version of the Sasquatch.

Before the end of the war, the British Army had introduced the Symien sniper suit,

Painters' Contribution to Camouflage

Notable among the pioneers of German camouflage was Franz Marc, a painter who was conscripted in 1914. Within two years he had been transferred to camouflage operations, experimenting with different styles in order to best hide artillery emplacements from aerial observation. Marc produced camouflage materials using a painting style called pointillism, consisting of many small dots. He was ordered to be withdrawn from combat duty in order to protect his contribution to the war effort, but was killed in action before receiving the order.

Meanwhile, the French painter Lucien-Victor Guirand de Scévola experimented with camouflage on his own artillery piece while serving in the French Army. His method, as befitted a pastellist, was to paint a canvas screen to hide his gun. His work came to the notice of the high command, and by early 1915 he was part of the Section de Camouflage. Later that year, Scévola was made commander of the Camouflage Corps. He is credited with the invention of camouflage netting.

The French army brought in painters, notably Cubists, to design its camouflage, and also built camouflaged observation posts disguised as trees. As many as 3,000 camouflage experts were under the command of Scévola by the early months of 1917; a nation that had gone to war convinced that red trousers were essential to military success had truly embraced the concept of concealment.

essentially making the Ghillie suit a formally recognized piece of military equipment. The Ghillie suits remain a part of sniper equipment to this day, and learning how to make an effective one is a vital part of sniper training.

Experiments towards the end of the war gave rise to the 'brushstroke' method of creating camouflage. This technique used large, irregular brushes to paint suitable colours onto a base material. The brushstrokes were irregular in shape, creating a disruptive pattern that influenced many later forms of camouflage.

This method was later used by British Major Denison to create the camouflage pattern associated with the 'Denison smock', an overgarment originally designed to be stepped into but later revised so that it was put on over the head. The Denison smock was extensively used throughout World War II, notably by airborne troops. It remained in service with the

British Army into the 1970s. The exact date of its withdrawal from service is hard to pin down but was probably some time in 1977. By the beginning of the 1980s, Denison smocks had been replaced by disruptive pattern uniforms.

The US Army adopted a sniper suit similar to the British Symien suit but also created suits specifically designed to provide concealment when hiding among trees. Interest waned after the end of the Great War, and though some experimentation was undertaken it was not until the entry of the US into World War II that camouflage became a serious concern again.

Camouflage in the Interwar Years

This was generally the way of things in the interwar years. Lessons learned were not so much forgotten as regarded as being of low priority. Another war on the scale of 1914–18 was all but unthinkable, and preparing for it

Above: In its present circumstances this 1917 US camouflage suit is rather obvious, not least due to the shadow cast by the wearer. However, at a distance, in poor light or against a cluttered backdrop this suit would make it hard to discern the wearer's body shape, and would make targeting more difficult if he were spotted at all.

was thus an uncomfortable prospect. Besides, with huge amounts of legacy equipment left over from the Great War and tough economic conditions to contend with, there was little funding for new equipment. However, some advances were made.

Germany took the idea of infantry camouflage sufficiently seriously to undertake a great deal of interwar experimentation. Advances in weaving technology permitted the creation of mass-produced camouflaged cloth, which was produced in a wide array of designs. Speckles, blotches and irregular stripes not dissimilar to brushstroke-style camouflage were all produced. Initially, camouflage clothing

was issued only to SS units, although after the outbreak of World War II all formations gradually received it.

The Italian Army adopted a camouflaged shelter-half in 1929, which was possibly the first mass-produced camouflage item for infantrymen (a shelter-half is a tarpaulin that can be used as a rain cape, or combined with another to make a two-man tent – hence its name). The German army followed suit in 1931, and later based their camouflage uniforms on patterns developed for the shelters.

A camouflaged shelter-half not only made troops in bivouac less conspicuous but also could be used as personal camouflage. Its loose shape softened the outlines of the soldier and his weapon, greatly reducing detectability. The concept is still in use today, although not all forces adopted the camouflaged version.

The earliest mass-produced camouflage garment issued to British forces arrived around 1930. It was designated 'Cape, Anti-Gas, No.1,

Camouflaged' and consisted of a knee-length smock of khaki cotton with irregular brown patches. Originally these garments were fairly dark due to the linseed oil used to waterproof them. Many surviving examples have faded as the oil leached out, creating a paler garment that may seem like desert camouflage. In fact, the No.1 cape was designed with the north European environment in mind. At roughly the same time, the British Army also introduced a groundsheet that could be used as a rain cape in the same camouflage pattern as the smock.

Axis Camouflage in World War II

The last years before the outbreak of war in 1939 were a curious mix of preparation and denial. The horrors and the appalling death toll of the Great War were recent memories; in addition, many people were convinced that any new war would see the almost immediate destruction of all major cities by waves of bombers. Rearmament came late in many nations, and was often rushed and inefficient. Almost everything was in short supply, and many good ideas were not implemented for lack of resources. Others were passed over as seemingly unnecessary in the sort of war that was expected, if it came at all. In some cases there was a reluctance to make preparations at all, since this was an admission that another Great War might actually happen.

The rearmament race was led (and arguably, triggered) by Germany, whose forces understood the benefits of camouflage. During the Great War, often the only part of a man visible above the trench parapet was his head. Steel helmets (stahlhelm) were introduced in 1916 to protect against

Left: A German SS soldier takes prisoner two Soviet tank crew following the fighting at Kursk, July 1943. Both the SS summer camouflage pattern smock and the Red Army's khaki uniform provided good concealment amidst the yellow wheatfields of a Russian summer.

Above: The Wehrmacht soldier (left) wears a simple *feldgrau* uniform, whereas the SS machine-gun team (above) have been issued camouflage clothing. It is, however, debatable which is better camouflaged at any given range; green-grey disappears into the background at a surprisingly short distance.

shell fragmentation, but their distinctive shape drew rifle fire. German soldiers learned to paint their helmets in camouflage colours to reduce their visibility.

Much of the effort expended in this direction was on an ad hoc basis, with individuals basing their camouflage on personal observation. There were, however, formally sanctioned camouflage experts within the German army. These experts, like those of other nations, were often painters.

EARLY GERMAN CAMOUFLAGE PATTERNS

Whether shooting, observing or just moving around in the trench, experience indicated that a low-visibility helmet offered real benefits, and as the German Army expanded in the 1930s camouflage equipment was deemed desirable. The first items went into

production in 1931, printed in a pattern known as *Heeres Splittermuster-31* (army splinter pattern). Among the equipment featuring this pattern was the *Zeltbahn-31*, a shelter-quarter printed with the same pattern but in different colouration on each side. *Heeres Splittermuster-31* was used for a number of army uniform designs. A variant was adopted by the Luftwaffe, while the *Zeltbahn* was produced in many variations. These included different camouflage colouring as well as variations on the fastenings and fittings.

The *Zeltbahn* was issued with a field manual detailing its many uses, as a shelter-quarter, a rain poncho or a camouflage item. Several *Zeltbahns* could be buttoned together to create quite large structures, including a 'house tent' made from 16 *Zeltbahns*. As a garment, a *Zeltbahn* could be buttoned in various ways to accommodate use on horseback or a bicycle, or could be worn over the top of equipment by an infantryman.

All personnel were issued a *Zeltbahn* (in theory at least; supplies of all items could be patchy at times), which was typically carried rolled and strapped horizontally across the back of the belt. It could also be wrapped around a mess tin or attached to a pack. After the Y-belt style webbing was issued to infantrymen in 1939, it became quite common to carry the *Zeltbahn* high on an infantryman's shoulders.

It was also possible to cut up a *Zeltbahn* and use it to create a camouflage jacket or smock. Early in World War II, only the Waffen-SS was issued camouflage uniforms. Wehrmacht infantrymen who desired concealment were

Below: Numerous camouflage patterns were used by the Axis forces in World War II. From left to right: *Platanenmuster* (plane tree pattern) was a dotted pattern available in spring/summer and autumn/winter variants, whilst *Splittertarn* used more angular shapes. Italian designers drew on World War I experience and produced a *Telo mimetico* using softer shapes.

forced to improvise, and the Zeltbahn provided a ready-made source of camouflage material.

WEHRMACHT AND SS UNIFORMS

The uniforms used by the Wehrmacht and the SS began to diverge around 1935, initially by way of fairly small stylistic changes but quite radically after a while. The typical German infantryman began World War II in a grey *Feldbluse* (field tunic). This was designated M36, but had its origins in a project implemented by the Weimar republic before the Nazi Party gained power. The new uniform was remodelled to accommodate motorized transport, with shorter tunic skirts, but retained the traditional field grey colouring.

The M36 tunic was originally worn with slate-grey trousers. These were officially replaced in 1940 with field grey, although the older trousers continued to be issued for some time. Similarly, the uniform as a whole evolved throughout the war, although the only major change was the introduction of a new M44 tunic that was shorter and easier to manufacture. The M44 tunic used a more brownish variant of *feldgrau*, but was

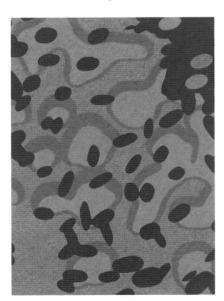

introduced too late to see widespread issue. Some newly raised formations received it, as did elements of the Volkssturm militia fielded towards the end of the war.

Although the field grey uniform offered a degree of reduced visibility, it was not camouflage as such. Helmets were often disguised by adding wire or netting into which vegetation or scraps of cloth were twined. As previously noted, Wehrmacht troops could use their *Zeltbahn* as a camouflage poncho, or modify it to create a camouflage garment.

The original *Splittermuster* pattern was joined by others as the war went on. A *Sumpfmuster* (swamp pattern) appeared in 1943 as a variant of the *Splittermuster*. Its shapes were later altered while retaining the colouration. A *Leibermuster*

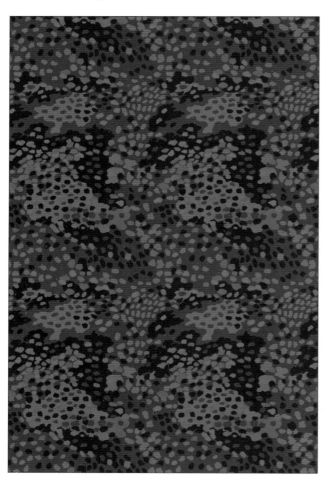

(leaf pattern) camouflage appeared too late in the war to be introduced on a widespread basis. *Leibermuster* camouflage was intended for use by both Wehrmacht and SS troops.

The SS was issued camouflage uniforms from an early date. Initially a block pattern was used, and was issued on a limited basis during 1936–38. More widespread was the *Platanenmuster* (plane tree) pattern, which was issued from 1936 to 1944. Based on the colours and shapes of the sycamore tree, this pattern was produced double-sided, with 'spring' and 'autumn' colouration.

Most of the camouflage used by the SS is credited to Johann Georg Otto Schick, about whom little is known. Schick is said to have come up with the idea of reversible camouflage clothing featuring spring and autumn patterns on opposite sides. His designs were patented, which permitted the SS to deny their use to the Wehrmacht. This sort of rivalry and internal empire building was rife within the Nazi Reich, and in this case allowed the SS to set themselves apart from (and presumably above) the ordinary soldiers of the Wehrmacht.

SS camouflage equipment included helmet covers as well as smocks and the ubiquitous cape/shelter-quarter. Most patterns were used for a variety of items, although there were exceptions. *Palmenmuster* (palm tree pattern) was produced during 1940–42 and was primarily issued to troops involved in the invasion of Russia. It was not used to produce Zeltbahns but exclusively for personal camouflage items such as helmet covers.

Left: *Erbsenmuster* **(pea dot pattern), designed by Johann Georg Otto Schick, was widely worn by Waffen-SS troops during the summer and autumn of 1944. In style, the pea dot was a major change from the earlier camouflage smocks. The two piece uniform was designed to be worn over the wool service uniform, or by itself.**

Rauchtarnmuster (blurred edge or smoke pattern) camouflage was produced between 1939 and 1944. This was a version of the earlier plane tree pattern overprinted in diffuse black. Introduced in 1941 and in production until 1945, the *Eichenlaubenmuster* (oak leaf pattern) saw widespread use for a variety of garments as well as shelters.

DEVELOPMENTS IN THE LATER WAR YEARS

Most, but not all, German camouflage items were reversible. The *Erbsenmuster* (pea pattern) introduced in 1944 was not, as it was intended for year-round use. Pea-pattern camouflage uniforms were produced as a smock and trousers and strongly influenced postwar designs. So did the *Leibermuster* (leaf pattern) camouflage introduced at the very end of the war. This was a six-colour pattern intended to incorporate a measure of infrared camouflage, but it arrived too late to be issued in any volume.

German units were at times issued Italian camouflage captured after Italy's surrender to the Allies in 1943. This was used to create a wide range of garments and camouflage items, many of them unorthodox or non-standard. This *Telo mimetico* was introduced in 1929 and remained in Italian service until the end of the 1980s, although the colouration was altered at times.

In most countries, airborne and parachute troops were part of the army, but Nazi Germany went down a different route. This was in part due to the will of Hermann

Left: The *Hermann Göring* Division had a complex history which resulted in it being transferred to the Luftwaffe when Göring was given command of that arm. Although it was an SS panzer formation it was designated a paratroop unit. The Luftwaffe had its own variant of the *Splittertarn* camouflage pattern.

Infantry Uniforms in World War II

Few nations began World War II with much camouflage equipment on issue to their forces. Specialist and elite units generally received camouflage, or forces operating in theatres where it seemed most beneficial.

German Infantryman (1940)
The early-war *feldgrau* uniform of the Wehrmacht reflects a move towards mechanised warfare. A short jacket is less encumbering when moving in and out of vehicles.

Belgian Infantryman (1940)
The Belgian Army began the war wearing uniforms somewhat French in style and had little chance to develop new equipment during the conflict.

British Commando (1942)
A simple khaki battledress offered good concealment during night raids at which the commando forces fielded by Britain excelled.

Italian 184th Parachute Division (1942)
Parachute troops, seen as elite forces in all nations, were often the first to receive camouflage as standard issue. Italy, like many nations, provided a camouflage smock worn over conventional combat dress.

German Infantryman (1943)

The rapid change in colouration between autumn, winter and spring caused many nations – including Germany – to issue reversible coveralls.

US 2nd Marine Division (1943)

The US Marine Corps experimented with camouflage equipment during the island-hopping warfare in the Pacific theatre. The difference in terrain between assault beaches and inland combat zones proved to be a problem.

German *Hitlerjügend* Division (1944)

After the surrender of Italy, many German units received equipment produced for the Italian army. The *Hitlerjügend* division was one such recipient of Italian pattern camouflage smocks.

US 1st Infantry Division (1944)

US troops taking part in the Normandy landings were in some cases equipped with camouflage gear. This caused some to be mistaken for SS troops, the main users of camouflage in the European theatre.

Above: The US Marines used dogs to flush out hidden Japanese snipers. They are wearing the two-piece camouflage uniform, which replaced the rather less convenient one-piece coverall originally issued.

Göring, who possessed sufficient influence to take control of parachute operations once Germany was prepared to openly admit it had an air force. The SS did create a small paratroop force, and the army fielded an air-mobile contingent, but the *Fallschirmjaeger* (paratroop) units were part of the Luftwaffe.

Towards the very end of the war, additional divisions that were ostensibly *Fallschirmjaeger* units were flung together from Luftwaffe personnel, although these were never intended to undertake airborne operations. They were simply expedient infantry forces created in response to a rapidly deteriorating situation. *Fallschirmjaeger* used a splinter-pattern

camouflage smock known as a *Knochensack* (bonesack), which was worn over other equipment. This characteristic garment and the tenacity of the elite paratroop units earned them the nickname 'Green Devils'. The Luftwaffe infantry formations created later were given a much more basic camouflage jacket, since the *Knochensack* was expensive and slow to produce.

The camouflage smock worn by *Fallschirmjaeger* influenced the development of paratroop equipment used in other nations, including the British Denison smock.

Allied Camouflage in World War II

Following the early years where olive drab and khaki were the norm, Allied camouflage developed rapidly, especially for special forces, such as paratroopers, commandos and the US Marine Corps.

US CAMOUFLAGE

The US Army made some use of personal camouflage during World War II, issuing a one-piece jungle camouflage uniform in 1942 and a two-piece version the year after. The nature of the war in the Pacific required soldiers to use light tan camouflage for operations on or near a landing beach and darker green equipment for operations inland. The issued uniform was thus reversible for these applications rather than the spring/autumn colouration common in Europe.

The one-piece camouflage suit was a clever design, intended to provide good ventilation and insect protection. It was loose-fitting to reduce chafing but was very heavy when wet. This, along with the general inconvenience of wearing a one-piece uniform with a pack over it, led to the introduction of the two-piece version. This in turn was modified in 1944, using darker colours. All versions of the uniform were constructed from herringbone twill (HBT).

The US Marine Corps made greater use of camouflage equipment, starting with the same one-piece jungle camouflage suit developed for the Army. By mid-1942, helmet covers of the same reversible material as the uniform were standard issue. The helmet cover received a slight upgrade in 1944 with the addition of pre-cut slits for the attachment of foliage.

While other nations were making increased use of personal camouflage, the US Army considered that it was actually less effective for many purposes. For those requiring static concealment, such as snipers and observers,

Left: The US military favoured a plain olive drab uniform for field operations, believing that camouflage patterns could actually be counterproductive when troops were on the move. Paratroopers of the 101st Airborne (left) were among the first troops into occupied Europe and were expected to be part of a rapid advance.

personal camouflage offered many advantages. However, for personnel whose role involved a lot of tactical movement (such as the majority of infantrymen), the US Army reverted to a plain olive drab uniform. Most troops later in the war were dressed in some variant of the 'Jacket, Field, M1943', an olive drab outer jacket with various inner layers depending on temperature conditions.

The decision not to use camouflage was not just about protecting US troops from enemy fire. The Second Armoured Division was issued a two-piece camouflage uniform for their part in the Normandy invasion. However, Allied troops were unused to seeing camouflage on their own side and assumed the wearers were SS soldiers and fired upon them.

Issue of camouflage equipment was always patchy due to the sheer amount required. A camouflaged shelter-half/rain poncho was produced in the same pattern as uniforms but was sometimes issued to units that had not received camouflage uniforms, and vice versa.

BRITISH CAMOUFLAGE

The British Army issued camouflage equipment before the outbreak of war, but in general personnel outside elite formations wore plain uniforms. There were exceptions; many units stationed in Belgium in the winter of 1944–45 were issued windproof camouflage smocks largely due to the extremely cold weather.

The battledress worn by most British soldiers was, like many uniforms of the era, designed with regard to movement in vehicles. It was also constructed so as not to impede the sort of movements an infantry soldier

Left: The British military issued the camouflaged Denison smock to airborne troops, including glider-borne forces, such as the pilot-officer featured here.

Above: Denison smock, 1944 pattern. The Denison smock remained in service in the British Army until the 1970s.

would be likely to make, such as aiming a rifle when kneeling or prone. Its colour came from a mix of green and brown fibres that created a reasonable approximation of Northern European vegetation. Battledress was issued from 1939 onwards, although some units were still wearing the older service dress at the outbreak of war. Battledress was copied wholesale by some other countries, while aspects of the design influenced military clothing in other nations. For example, the 'Ike' jacket used by US personnel was derived from the British version.

Units issued camouflage equipment – typically elite formations such as parachutists and commandos, or specialists such as snipers – usually wore a smock and pants over their

Right: British forces fighting in the Far East used a jungle green uniform matched to the prevailing colour of the terrain. Jungle fighting was often claustrophobic, with threats emerging suddenly and sources of fire hard to pinpoint. The conditions took a rapid toll on men and equipment, with moisture being a particular problem.

British Camofleurs

Much of the British body of knowledge used in World War II was based on the work of Hugh Bamford Cott, whose book *Adaptive Coloration in Animals* was published in 1940. Cott made an extensive study of camouflage in nature, covering similar ground to Thayer but also including measures such as lures and decoys, misdirection and the presentation of a false impression of strength.

Cott was a student of John Graham Kerr, and espoused many of his ideas. He was also a soldier, and had served as a camouflage expert between 1919 and 1922. Cott advocated the use of the same principles that were at play in nature, including countershading as first put forward by Thayer. He demonstrated the principle by camouflaging two identical artillery pieces, one with conventional camouflage and the other using countershading. The conventionally camouflaged gun was not hard to make out in photographs, whereas the countershaded one was all but invisible.

Despite this, Cott was not able to convince the British military to adopt his ideas, and in 1940 he resigned from the Camouflage Advisory Panel.

Geoffrey Barkas was a film-maker who was trained as a camouflage expert upon joining the British Army in 1940. He challenged the complacent attitude many soldiers had about their camouflage netting, demonstrating that it was not, as he called it, a 'cloak of invisibility' and was in fact useless if improperly applied. His inventive method of getting the message across was a poem called *The Sad Story of George Nathaniel Glover.* This Glover was an army driver who did not conceal his vehicle and was eventually bombed into oblivion.

Barkas brought his skills as a film director to bear on the problem of getting the camouflage message over, staging demonstrations in which an aircraft would be sent to look for vehicles that had just been camouflaged in front of visiting officers. Having seen the effectiveness of camouflage applied right before their eyes, the observers were more likely to promote its use in their own units. He also put forward what seems today to be obvious but that was not widely recognized at the time; that every region has a natural colouration and patterning.

Barkas was transferred to North Africa, where he published a manual entitled *Concealment in the Field*, which became required reading for officers in all units. In the meantime he headed a camouflage training camp, where Cott served as his head instructor. The camouflage patterns used by Barkas and his subordinates were based on first-hand observations of the terrain and conditions, notably from the air.

The crowning achievement of Barkas and his team was an immense deception operation undertaken before the battle of El Alamein (see Chapter 3). An entire dummy army was created, then replaced with a combat-ready one once the enemy had been allowed to realize that what they faced was not a real force. The surprise thus achieved contributed enormously to victory at El Alamein.

Right: The Soviet armed forces frequently had to operate in snowy conditions even before Russia became involved in World War II. Lessons were learned from the 'Winter War' with Finland in 1939–40, and effective winter camouflage was put in place throughout the Red Army.

battledress. The standard camouflage smock used by British personnel was designed by Major Denison and appeared in several variants – some of them local expedients – throughout the war.

A new version of the Denison smock appeared in 1944, featuring a different colour scheme matched to the conditions on Continental Europe. In the meantime, an alternative garment made from denim had been brought into service in 1942. Unlike the Denison smock, this 'Smock, Windproof, 1942 Pattern' was not designed with the needs of parachutists in mind. It had a hood, and was issued to snipers and other specialist infantry as well as commandos and raiders.

The Denison smock was also used by agents of the Special Operations Executive, along with a jumpsuit in green or white camouflage. These garments were intended to help an operative hide after landing by parachute in occupied territory. Operatives got rid of their camouflage materials – which would instantly mark them as foreign agents – as soon as they were able, adopting a different protective colouration in the form of a cover identity and the appearance of an innocent local person.

SOVIET CAMOUFLAGE

The armed forces of Russia appreciated the value of deception and concealment, and wartime sources state that camouflage was taught from the very first day of a soldier's training. Indeed, it may have been considered more important than weapons handling; units whose overall standard and combat capabilities were very low still attracted comment from foreign observers about the seriousness with which they treated camouflage.

The Soviet armed forces operated in a variety of conditions, from Europe to the Far East, and often in arctic conditions. This necessitated a variety of camouflage materials, most of which were based on the fairly standard smocks and helmet covers used elsewhere. In addition, Soviet riflemen were issued a small camouflage net that could be garnished with locally obtained foliage.

Camouflage materials were issued primarily to specialists including snipers and observers but also signallers and field engineers. Other personnel had plain uniforms that offered the same relatively low visibility as those used in other nations, and were expected to camouflage themselves with whatever materials they could obtain.

During and immediately after the German invasion of Russia in 1941, several pamphlets and manuals were published that detailed the camouflage methods encountered. The German

army was clearly impressed and more than a little alarmed by the Russian talent for concealment.

Among the techniques used were ready-made camouflage carpets with strands of different colours woven through them; wire frames to support camouflage materials in front of a rifle or machine-gun position; and an array of nets and fringes to support locally sourced materials. More importantly, the Soviet infantryman was indoctrinated to make good use of concealment at every opportunity.

The earliest Soviet camouflage garment was the ZMK arctic camouflage overgarment, first

Below: Winter camouflage cannot be pure white or it will stand out against the snow. A greyish or off-white colour is better, possibly with patches of green, black or grey. In an open, snow-covered landscape enemy personnel are particularly vulnerable to the sniper who is willing to remain still and wait for targets despite the cold.

issued in 1937 or 1938. Non-arctic personal camouflage generally used an 'amoeba' pattern of irregular blotches. Spring and summer patterns were generally more green and autumn colours were tan or brown, with all-white, white-on-green and green-on-white for snowy conditions. Camouflage was issued as one-piece coveralls or a smock and pants in most cases, often carried in a bag made from the same coloured material that could be used as an additional piece of camouflage.

The one-piece camouflage suit was named *makirovochnyi kombinezon* (MK); the two-piece version was designated *makrirovochnyi kamuflirovannyi kostium* (MKK). Colouration varied not only in an attempt to match the various conditions encountered by the Red Army, but also due to inconsistency between factories turning out the huge numbers of camouflage uniforms required. One deliberate variation appeared in 1941. Named *letniy kamuflyazh*, or 'summer camouflage', this design was produced in green or greyish-brown and was in some cases reversible.

In addition to the use of camouflage on a personal scale or to conceal positions, the Soviet Army made extensive use of natural masking for its personnel and positions. Soldiers who had constructed camouflaged positions or shelters were expected to remain in them during daylight, and were punished if they did not.

The Red Army was probably the greatest exponent of camouflage throughout World War II, evolving a doctrine that did not merely enforce the use of camouflage for concealment

purposes but included many inventive ways to exploit the advantage thus gained. It was noted with some alarm by German officers involved in Operation Barbarossa in 1941 that a Russian infantryman hiding under a camouflage carpet was virtually invisible unless all but stepped upon. Coupled with a willingness to wait until an enemy advance had gone past their positions before opening fire, this made Russian infantry – even low-quality units – extremely dangerous.

CHAPTER 2

INFANTRY CAMOUFLAGE IN THE MODERN ERA

Camouflage is an integral part of modern warfare; so much so that it is easy to forget there was a time when this was not the case.

There are many possible definitions of exactly when the 'modern era' of warfare began, but the end of World War II serves as a useful starting point. By the end of that conflict, warfare had advanced enormously; concepts that were experimental in 1939 were routine in 1945.

The battlefield had become a different and altogether more dangerous place, with far more automatic weapons and additional threats from tanks and aircraft. These had all existed before 1939, but by the end of the war the combination of rapid mechanized advances and heavy air support had changed the nature of conflict. Urban warfare had become commonplace, creating a new and extremely dangerous theatre for combat. It was also widely supposed that

Opposite: Even knowing that there is a sniper team in this picture, it can be difficult at first glance to make them out or determine which way they are facing. Good camouflage does not merely blend and disguise, it robs the eye of reference points.

the atomic bomb had rendered conventional conflict obsolete. Surely no major war could be fought in an environment where utter annihilation was possible?

Despite the rapidly increasing number of atomic weapons available, large-scale conventional conflict erupted almost immediately. The Chinese Civil War, which had been ongoing since 1926 but was interrupted by the Japanese invasion in 1937, resumed once Japan had been defeated. China was eventually united under a Communist government, but in the meantime displaced people spilled over into neighbouring countries. This contributed to the Malayan Emergency of 1948–60 and influenced other regional conflicts.

The Korean Conflict

The arbitrary partition of Korea into the Russian-influenced (and therefore Communist) North and Western-aligned South resulted in an attempt to reunify the country under the

Above: During the Korean Conflict, the US Marine Corps reverted to a plain drab uniform. Camouflage-patterned helmet covers were also used.

Communist North. The Korean Conflict (there was no declared war) initially went very well for North Korea, which was heavily armed with equipment that had been left behind by Russian forces. South Korea was woefully unprepared, and was all but overrun before a US-led international response restored the situation. This in turn brought in China on the North Korean side, resulting in a stalemate that eventually became an uneasy armistice.

The Korean conflict was in many ways the first of the 'limited wars' of the Cold War era, in that although China was a belligerent its involvement was limited; the international forces opposing North Korea were forced to take steps to avoid escalation that might lead to full Chinese involvement. Chinese aircraft that ventured over Korea were fair game, but could not be pursued north of the Yalu River; nor could their bases be attacked.

Yet despite a very different world political situation from the total war that had just finished, the Korean conflict was fought with equipment constructed for World War II and using tactics proven in that conflict. Among them was the use of 'garnish' – typically pieces of vegetation taken from the immediate surroundings to supplement or create camouflage. Garnish was particularly important in altering the appearance of a helmet; nets to hold twigs, leaves and rags of the correct colour were issued even by nations that did not otherwise provide troops with camouflage equipment.

The Buildup to the Cold War

Other aspects of the early Cold War era had their origins in World War II. Communist influences and a weakening of the colonial powers prompted several regions to seek national independence. France lost its colonies

Above: Soviet soldiers during the invasion of Czechoslovakia in 1968 wore the same khaki brown uniforms as their World War II forebears.

in Southeast Asia after a conflict that might be considered the first modern insurgency. Despite superior technology, the French were defeated, paving the way for Communism to spread throughout Southeast Asia and eventually to draw the US into a highly asymmetric war in Vietnam.

The concept of asymmetric warfare, which pits a technologically advanced force against a much lower-tech one, is well known today, but in the postwar world the developed nations had just emerged from a conflict that was very different. World War II was characterized by advanced (for the time) technology on all sides, clashes between massed forces and the rise of large-scale mechanized air/land warfare. This led to a style of thinking that was not entirely appropriate to some of the postwar conflicts.

An enemy that would not concentrate and fight in a manner that maximized the effects of artillery, air power and armour had to be fought on a man-to-man basis. Technological advantages were of varying usefulness in these conflicts, while the Mk1 Infantryman remained the most reliable weapon against dispersed opponents. Many of the postwar conflicts were counterinsurgency campaigns or drawn-out security operations against an enemy who would rarely stand and fight. In this new combat environment, personal camouflage was more important than ever.

At the same time, tension between the former Allies increased until the situation resembled an armed standoff. Agreements made in the closing months of World War II now caused additional complexities. Berlin was divided into zones controlled by the Soviet Union and the Western Allies, and was ultimately partitioned by the infamous Berlin Wall. West Berlin, although garrisoned by American, British and French troops, lay within East Germany, which was under the domination of the Soviet Union.

Politically, the option to withdraw from West Berlin did not exist. But with access limited to a narrow corridor – which was shut off in June 1948 – the situation was very difficult. The closing of all road, rail and waterway links was intended to force West Berlin to join East Berlin, but ultimately failed. The city was kept supplied by the greatest airlift operation in history, and ultimately remained Western territory.

Cold War Tensions

Tensions of this sort characterized the Cold War, and was one reason why the Soviet Union maintained large bodies of border and political troops. They were also useful for dealing with dissent within the Soviet Union and among its allies. The formation of the North Atlantic Treaty Organisation (NATO) in 1949 was not directed specifically against the Soviet Union, but the implications were obvious. When West Germany joined NATO in 1955, the Soviet Union formalized its own alliances with the Warsaw Pact.

It was obvious that in any clash between NATO and the Warsaw Pact, Germany would be the primary battleground. West Germany was permitted to rearm its forces but could not hope to defend its territory against the Warsaw Pact: a repeat of the 'Red Steamroller' of 1944–45 was likely. NATO forces were stationed in Germany but the complex political situation of the time was such that it was not possible to redeploy these formations to create a more effective defence. Treaties made at the end of World War II essentially required NATO troops in West Germany to be based wherever they had ended the war. They were also limited in numbers.

Tensions ran high for many years, especially when the Warsaw Pact intervened in Hungary to

Above: The US military gained extensive experience of operating in forested or jungle terrain during World War II. Mitchell Pattern camouflage was well suited to such terrain, making use of mixed dark and lighter tones on a tan background.

put down a revolution against the Communist ruling party and later invaded Czechoslovakia to halt a reform process that might have threatened Czechoslovakia's status as a Warsaw Pact member. Warsaw Pact backing for Communist revolutionaries worldwide, but especially in South America, also increased the possibility of World War III.

If such tensions had spilled over into open war, the decisive theatre would have been the Northern European Plain and the dense urban areas of Germany. This created quite different camouflage needs; one based on traditional temperate-vegetation patterns and the other more suited to urban conflict. The latter was used more for vehicles and installations than personnel.

Later in the Cold War era, the increasing use of night vision equipment and infrared

Right: The ERDL camouflage pattern was developed for jungle terrain, and underwent field trials during the Vietnam War. Early production suffered from roller slippage, which could cause inconsistencies in the pattern or areas that were not correctly printed.

cameras prompted research into camouflage that might help personnel evade detection by these devices or at least make them a more difficult target for enemies using them. Not all of these experiments were a success, but some formed the basis of advanced modern camouflage systems.

Pacific and Asian Influences on Camouflage

The camouflage patterns inherited by the US Army at the end of World War II were mainly those used by the Marine Corps in the Pacific. A reversible design, sometimes referred to as 'frogskin' or 'duck hunter', was used for various camouflage clothing and equipment such as parachutes. These items had a three-colour brown ('beach') pattern on one side with a five-colour green ('jungle') pattern on the other.

Camouflage-patterned parachutes were phased out towards the end of the 1950s, but the cloth was put to other – often unauthorized – uses by personnel in the field. Helmet covers and improvised camouflage blankets were made by many troops and were generally well regarded. These improvised items remained in use – at least with some personnel – even after regulation camouflage equipment became available.

In the late 1940s and early 1950s, the US military made a study of camouflage requirements and produced new designs, not all of which were implemented at the time. The US Marine Corps received a camouflaged shelter-half in 1953 and a helmet cover in 1959

that used a reversible vine (or wine) leaf pattern using shapes similar to twigs and leaves. The Mitchell pattern appeared at around the same time and featured a green 'leaf' pattern on one side and a brown 'cloud' pattern on the other.

In the meantime, the US Army developed a jungle pattern camouflage normally referred to as ERDL, after the Engineer Research and Development Laboratory, but sometimes called 'leaf pattern' by the personnel who wore it. ERDL used a light green background overlaid with darker green and brown shapes, but was not implemented at the time. It was re-evaluated in 1962 and began field trials in 1966. US Marines and Special Forces units favoured the design, as did Australian and New Zealand units who encountered it. ERDL was widely copied and is still in use by some nations.

Most US personnel did not receive camouflage uniforms until the early 1980s, when a camouflaged battle dress uniform (BDU) was introduced as standard. The initial issue was for temperate climates, with tropical versions following later. BDUs remained in service for the next two decades, albeit with some revisions.

Above: 'Tiger-stripe' camouflage patterns, as worn by this Army of the Republic of Vietnam soldier, emerged during the Vietnam War, and were intended to disguise the characteristic shape of limbs and body using a horizontal patterning. The concept was sufficiently successful that several nations adopted this pattern.

Indochina Wars

The postwar development of camouflage by US forces was heavily influenced by experiences in the Pacific theatre of World War II, and later by the Korean conflict. Other nations were also influenced by their involvement in the region. French troops serving in their colonies in Southeast Asia used lizard pattern camouflage, and after the French withdrawal the Republic of Vietnam continued to use these designs.

Lizard pattern camouflage typically uses patches of two colours overlaid on a background colour, usually with a horizontal bias intended to break up the vertical body shape of the wearer. US special forces advising the South Vietnamese adopted these uniforms and evolved the design into a characteristic 'tiger-stripe' version.

Tiger-stripe was not officially issued by the US military, but was widely adopted by US, Australian and New Zealand special forces and elite units operating in Vietnam. It was eventually replaced in US service by ERDL designs, but in the meantime was used for a variety of camouflage items including hats. Tiger-stripe has been adopted by several militaries outside of Southeast Asia since the end of the Vietnam conflict.

The conflicts in French Indochina and later in Vietnam had their origin, to a great extent, in the Chinese Civil War and World War II. The Japanese occupation of what was then French Indochina was challenged from 1941 onwards by a Communist force that proclaimed independence at the end of the war. The area was still a French colonial possession at that time, and French forces attempted to reassert control of the region.

The result was an asymmetric conflict in which the French were eventually defeated. This led to the creation of a Communist state in

Above: The Mekong Delta region was characterised by patterns of light and shade caused by bright sunlight and tall vegetation, with areas of open water in between. Here, a US special forces soldier's 'tiger-stripe' pattern camouflage helps him easily blend in to the jungle foliage.

North Vietnam and a Westernized one in South Vietnam. When the latter was threatened with a Communist takeover, US forces were deployed to oppose the spread of Communism. Initially this intervention took the form of advisors and special forces personnel training local troops, but eventually expanded into a major war effort.

Camouflage in the Vietnam War

The Vietnam War was characterized by jungle terrain where ambush and counter-ambush were highly effective tactics. In some areas it was possible to fight a modern set-piece battle, and the US and South Vietnamese forces were highly successful in these actions. The role of the Viet

Cong guerrillas compared to the regular North Vietnamese Army is often overstated, especially in popular versions of the conflict such as movies, but concealment and camouflage played an important role in the conflict.

Concealment was used at all levels of the fighting, from hidden booby-traps to large-scale movement of supplies under the cover of the forest canopy. Snipers played an important part in the conflict on both sides, although they varied in capability from hidden riflemen whose skill might be lacking to legendary figures such as Gunnery Sergeant Carlos Hathcock. Hathcock was an extremely good shot, of course, but he was also a master of concealment.

Hathcock was involved in both countersniper and counter-countersniper operations, in which skilled snipers attempted to hunt and kill their opposite numbers. This was a very personal conflict amid a wider war, and was as much a battle of nerves and patience as of skill. Few personnel could affect the outcome of a conflict as much as a good sniper, so eliminating one who was thought to be in the area was a worthwhile, if dangerous, undertaking.

One important facet of countersniping operations was to figure out where the enemy sniper might hide. Good shooting positions are not obvious to non-snipers, but someone with equivalent training might be able to predict where the sniper would conceal himself. A very skilled sniper might take a less-than-ideal position precisely because his opponents would know where to look, but even if his position were correctly guessed he might still not be spotted.

The camouflage used by snipers was typically created on a personal basis, although use might be made of existing uniform items as a base. The knowledge gained by successful snipers was valuable to those researching better camouflage materials as they experienced it from both sides – the difficulty of spotting and hitting a target weighed against their own ability to avoid detection.

The US military emerged from Vietnam in the mid-1970s with a distinct sensation of burning fingers. Although every major action resulted in victory for US forces, and the Viet Cong was effectively broken from 1968 onwards, the war was lost at a political level and Vietnam ended up unified under a Communist government. Lessons were learned about the conduct of war in the modern world at many levels, including a wealth of experience about concealment and camouflage in the jungle environment.

Experiences in Africa

In the mid-20th century, Africa still had several colonial enclaves owned by European nations, and many emerging nations that had previously been colonial areas. Some of these developed their own military capabilities, drawing upon the doctrine and equipment of the former colonial powers. Others were influenced by the nations from which they sought help in their struggles for independence.

Among the colonial powers of Africa was Portugal, whose internal political troubles paved the way for independence among its colonies. In addition to insurgencies elsewhere, Portuguese forces became embroiled in a multi-way struggle for control of Angola, with several factions backed by other nations.

Portuguese troops serving in Africa used a vertical lizard pattern that influenced many of the forces fighting against them, while Cuban forces, which intervened in the conflict to assist the left-wing People's Movement for the Liberation of Angola (MPLA) faction, used a more

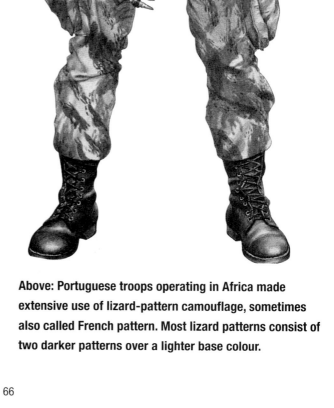

Above: Portuguese troops operating in Africa made extensive use of lizard-pattern camouflage, sometimes also called French pattern. Most lizard patterns consist of two darker patterns over a lighter base colour.

conventional horizontal lizard pattern largely derived from Soviet designs.

Lizard pattern camouflage was adopted by several factions as well as some of the African nations, and has come to be widely associated with African forces in general, despite originating in France. It has been used by nations as far afield as Israel and Russia, and remains in widespread service today.

Many of the conflicts in Africa during the Cold War era and afterwards were along tribal or factional lines rather than national ones. The forces of warlords and guerrilla movements have rarely been equipped in a uniform manner, and often wear civilian clothing with or without some distinguishing mark. Camouflage equipment, where it is used, tends to come from wherever it can be obtained – usually whichever nation feels that backing the faction is in its interests at the time.

Thus, African irregular forces tended not to drive the science of camouflage forward,

but instead used what was already available and adapt it as best they could. The armed forces of the major African nations grew in power and sophistication throughout the twentieth century and although they, too, as a rule followed developments implemented elsewhere, camouflage uniforms for infantry became commonplace.

Experiences in the Middle East

The Middle East is one of the most troubled regions of the world, and not coincidentally the Israeli Defence Force (IDF) is one of the most combat-experienced military forces of modern times. Originally equipped with World War II-era Western arms and uniforms, the IDF has fought several wars against its Arab

Below: The Israeli Defence Force possessed stocks of lizard pattern camouflage obtained from France. However, plain drab battle dress was considered the best for all-round use for the Middle Eastern battlefield.

The Benefits of Green as a Camouflage Colour

It has been suggested that since the human eye does not discern green very well in poor light or where visibility is not good, a plain green uniform might offer better concealment than a multicoloured one. Some observers have remarked how modern camouflage clothing can stand out under certain light conditions, whereas drab green fades into the background.

This concept is corroborated by data from motor insurance companies, whose studies have suggested that dull green cars are more likely to be involved in an accident at dawn or dusk than cars of any other colour.

neighbours and insurgent groups. Leaving aside all considerations of the region's politics, these conflicts have resulted in a wealth of practical experience that has influenced the development and procurement of Israeli arms and equipment.

The IDF did not follow the general move towards personal camouflage that was prevalent in the Cold War years. Instead, it stuck with an olive drab field uniform, with special forces using an array of camouflage equipment when necessary. The Israeli military has shown itself very willing to spend money on items considered necessary, yet a camouflage uniform for infantry personnel was not among them.

One possible reason for this is the same lesson that was learned by some US troops in the Pacific theatre during World War II. Camouflage is most effective when stationary, and thus very useful for installations, bunkers,

Above: During the conflict in Lebanon in the early 1980s, plain olive drab was worn by IDF troops. Since much of the fighting took place in an urban environment, 'natural' camouflage patterns would have been of little use.

Right: The Soviet armed forces were the first to experiment with digital designs, and later combined digital type with softer shapes. This veteran of the fighting in Afghanistan is presumably wearing the same pattern as he used in the conflict, but many different patterns were issued to the Red Army, not least because of the sheer number of troops to be equipped.

observers and snipers. But for infantrymen on the move, it can actually be more visible than a plain uniform.

There is also the possibility that since Israeli forces operated aboard or close to vehicles much of the time, personal camouflage was less important than concealing the vehicle. In an urban environment – where Israeli forces operate much of the time – camouflage designed to blend into the natural environment may be less useful.

This is not to say that the IDF does not believe in camouflage. Tents and similar equipment are produced in camouflage colours, and soldiers are trained to use foliage or naturally occurring dust for camouflage purposes. In many areas, anyone who drops to the ground to take cover is liable to be immediately covered with dust that is the same colour as the surroundings and thus is provided with effective personal camouflage by nature itself.

Soviet Cold War Camouflage

The Soviet armed forces received amoeba pattern camouflage during World War II, and this remained in service afterwards. It was phased out for most troops in the 1950s, but was issued (notably to new recruits) until the mid-1990s. Its replacement began to appear from 1940 onwards, using a leaf pattern that was also adopted by some Soviet allies. Other patterns were also issued, including a digital-type design named *tritsvetnyi makirovochnyi kamuflirovannyi kostium* (TTsMKK).

The Soviet armed forces continued to experiment with different designs including a cross between amoeba and TTsMKK, as well as various other leaf and geometrical patterns. The sheer numbers of uniforms produced during the war meant that older camouflage designs remained in use and were passed on to allied nations.

The Soviet armed forces made few revisions to their camouflage designs during the 1950s, but during the 1960s and early 1970s a new design of coverall designated *kamuflirovannyi letyni maskirovochniy kombinezon* (KLMK) was issued to high-end units such as airborne and special forces formations. KLMK used a 'spatter' pattern in grey on a green background and featured an integral hood with a facemask.

Another Soviet designs from this era was a desert camouflage system named *pustinoi maskirovchnyi kombinezon*, which used 'stair step' patterns. It soon disappeared, and may have been a trial version or a special issue for some personnel only. The *kostium zachchitnoi seti* (KZS) system appeared in 1975 and was apparently considered to be more or less disposable. It took the form of a loose-woven overgarment and was used in Afghanistan by combat engineers, among others, before being adopted by airborne troops.

Soviet equipment during this period was not of very high quality, but from the early 1980s onwards camouflage uniforms began to improve. By the time of the Soviet intervention in Afghanistan a new uniform was in use. This was of a better design, possibly influenced by Western combat equipment, and was more durable. It used a three-colour 'woodland' camouflage pattern that was quite different from Western camouflage of the same name.

'Stair step' re-emerged in 1981 in a format often associated with special forces, border guards and political troops. For this reason it is often referred to as 'special purpose' (*spetsodezhda*). Although widely rumoured to have been designed using digital methods, there is no evidence for this. This new uniform was of greatly improved cut and durability, and its pattern is still in use.

British and European Cold War Camouflage

British forces retained the Denison smock until the 1970s, but by the early 1960s moves were underway to create a camouflage uniform for all personnel. A Disruptive Pattern Camouflage

The Soviets in Afghanistan

The Soviet involvement in Afghanistan has been referred to as 'Russia's Vietnam'. The initial intervention met with relatively little resistance, not least due to clever deception operations that neutralized some of the Afghan forces before the invasion and the fact that the intervention was launched to assist a pro-Soviet government faction. However, despite securing the cities with relative ease, Soviet forces met with determined resistance from guerrillas, particularly along the land routes to Soviet territory.

The Soviet armed forces were not well prepared for this kind of war. The Red Army filled its ranks by conscription, with the best recruits being taken by specialist units. The remainder were mainly conscripts who often came from diverse ethnic backgrounds and spoke several different languages. Such raw material was perhaps suitable for massed action against NATO in northern Europe – if properly directed – but a counter-insurgency campaign required a different sort of soldier.

The Russian campaign in Afghanistan was characterized by guerrilla actions, notably against supply convoys moving along the few available roads from Russian territory to the Afghan cities. These routes were often flanked by high ground, creating a multitude of ambush points.

uniform was introduced in 1969 and was designated Pattern 1960 DPM. The '1960' in this case referred to the fact that the new uniform was a camouflage version of the olive drab one issued in 1960.

Similarly, the Pattern 1968 DPM uniform that followed was not issued to any great extent until 1970. It was followed a few years later by a tropical version. As in other nations, colour variance in these camouflage schemes was as often due to inconsistencies between manufacturers as deliberate policy changes.

While later uniforms improved on the materials and sometimes the design of the clothing, the DPM pattern camouflage remained more or less the same – albeit with colour changes to suit different environments. The 1984 Pattern uniform, for example, was influenced by experiences during the Falklands War of 1982 in terms of cut and design, but retained the traditional DPM camouflage. This has been widely copied and is one of the most enduring of all camouflage designs.

As noted elsewhere, French forces in Indochina made extensive use of lizard pattern camouflage, which was standardized in several colour schemes. This did not prevent experimentation; in the early 1980s, a number of camouflage schemes were trialled that were based on dots. Although not adopted for service, these proved influential and may have contributed to German 'Flecktarn' designs.

The term 'Flecktarn' comes from a conflation of 'fleck' (i.e. 'spot') and 'tarnung', the German word for camouflage. Flecktarn may have been influenced by wartime pea pattern (*Erbsenmuster*) designs, but this is doubtful. It was considered for a long time, beginning trials in 1976 and entering service in 1989. This coincided with major changes in the world political

Left: The Falklands War of 1982 took place in an environment characterised by cold moorland, not very different in colour and tone to some parts of Northern Europe. This British Special Boat Service soldier is wearing the standard DPM camouflage uniform of the period – perfect for reconnaissance and raiding missions.

Chronology of Modern Infantry Uniforms

After the end of World War II opinions were divided as to whether camouflage or plain uniforms offered better concealment. There was, however, a general move towards camouflage.

Foreign Legion Parachute Brigade (1952)

The French Foreign Legion adopted considerable amounts of US equipment, including camouflage jackets, in the post-war years.

Red Army private (1956)

In the early Cold War era, the huge Soviet army was made up largely of conscripts and given fairly basic equipment.

British SAS (1966)

Post-war, the Special Air Service made use of whatever equipment seemed useful or was available, including here a jungle green uniform of unidentified origin.

Israeli Golani Brigade (1967)

The Israeli Defence Force was still using lizard pattern camouflage into the late 1960s, but abandoned it by the end of the decade.

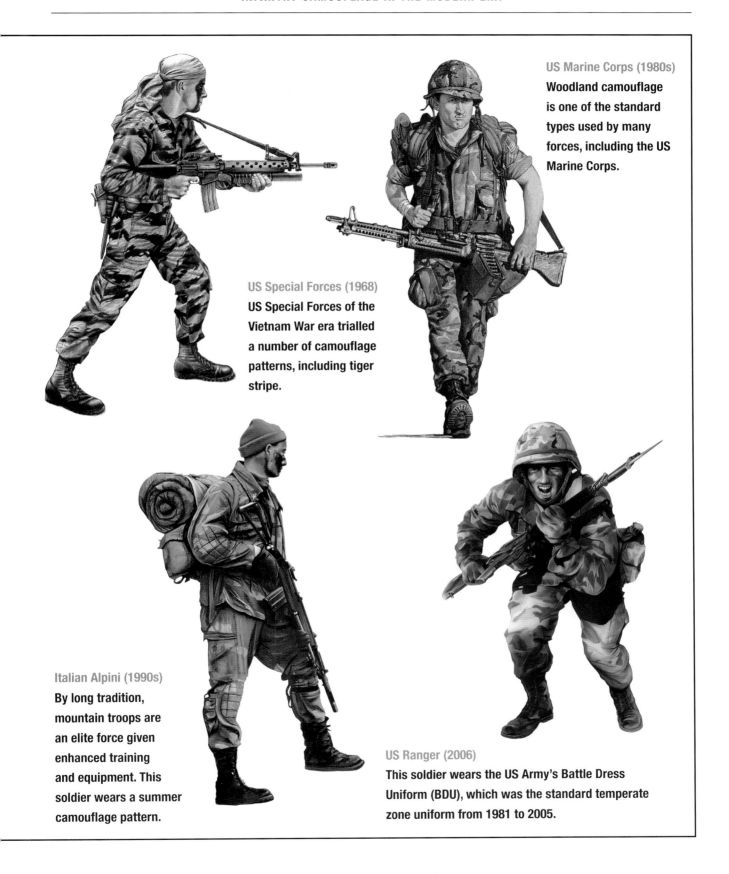

US Marine Corps (1980s)
Woodland camouflage is one of the standard types used by many forces, including the US Marine Corps.

US Special Forces (1968)
US Special Forces of the Vietnam War era trialled a number of camouflage patterns, including tiger stripe.

Italian Alpini (1990s)
By long tradition, mountain troops are an elite force given enhanced training and equipment. This soldier wears a summer camouflage pattern.

US Ranger (2006)
This soldier wears the US Army's Battle Dress Uniform (BDU), which was the standard temperate zone uniform from 1981 to 2005.

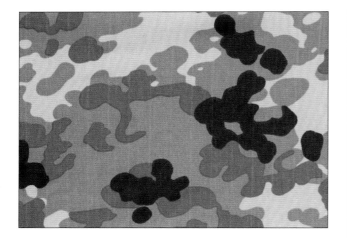

Above: Although developed in Germany, Flecktarn pattern camouflage has found favour elsewhere, such as with Japanese forces.

situation and a greater involvement of German forces in peacekeeping operations overseas.

After World War II, East Germany was part of the Soviet Bloc, while West Germany, although a NATO member from the mid-1950s, did not take part in overseas military operations. The needs of its armed forces were therefore geared to the defence of Germany itself. For this reason, pre-1990s German camouflage was almost exclusively matched to North European conditions.

Early in the Cold War era, the West German army received few camouflage items. Notable was a shelter-half in a reversible summer/autumn colour scheme. Helmet covers in the same 'Amoebatarn' design were produced in small numbers but were not widely issued. Snow camouflage (*Schneetarn*) was issued in the 1960s, in the form of a reversible coverall in all-white/white with green splodges. This was revised in the 1980s, but can still be encountered in service.

Other experiments were undertaken but it was not until the reunification of Germany in 1990, after which German forces began to

Above: These 1950s West German troops are equipped with legacy weapons from the World War II era, and wear winter camouflage drawing on experience in that conflict.

operate in a wider variety of environments, that a greater range of camouflage patterns was required. Once adopted, Flecktarn was thus issued in a variety of colour schemes and has been influential in other countries. Some, such as Poland, are closely related to Germany and have similar terrain conditions. Others, for example China, have adopted Flecktarn designs for operations in particular environments such as Tibet. It is unlikely that this would be done for political reasons, so presumably the Chinese military considers Flecktarn patterns to be the most effective in these regions.

The Post-Cold War World

Cold War-era conflicts such as the Falklands War made it clear that the polarization of world politics into essentially two huge power blocs – the Soviet-led Warsaw Pact and NATO – with China as a third and increasingly powerful player – had not made the military environment any less complex. The threat of a clash between the power blocs remained a possibility throughout the Cold War era, and the armed forces of both sides had to be ready to fight a major war in Europe, with additional actions in other theatres.

On the other hand, those same forces had to be able to deal with insurgencies and interventions elsewhere in the world, quite possibly switching from a major-war mindset to one of peacekeepers bound by rigid rules of engagement in a complex situation. In between these two scenarios lay the possibility of a war on a more limited scale than an all-out superpower confrontation. The personnel and equipment of the Cold War era had to be ready for almost

anything, almost anywhere. If anything, this situation has only become more complex.

The world political situation changed considerably at the beginning of the 1990s. The collapse of the Soviet Union resulted in the break-up of the Warsaw Pact and the appearance – in many cases reappearance – of many nations that had once been part of the Soviet Union. Freed of the tight control once exerted over them, many of these nations sought to chart their own path into the future. New alliances began to form, while rebel groups in many regions tried to create a homeland of their own out of the territory of emerging states.

Initially these new states were equipped with legacy equipment left over from the Cold War, and it was generally cost-effective and convenient

Below: Since the end of World War II, the People's Liberation Army of China has evolved rapidly, developing its own camouflage doctrine. Experiments with digital patterns have been undertaken alongside more conventional designs, such as this British-style DPM.

to follow previous designs and doctrine. Over time, however, these new states began to develop their own military systems or to obtain equipment from outside their old alliance.

At the same time, other nations emerged as major players in the post-Cold War world. China is now a superpower, and other nations such as India have greatly increased their influence. New power structures emerged from the Cold War world, and the global arms market changed significantly.

At the height of the Cold War, arms procurement was inextricably tied to politics. Few nations bought equipment (or were provided with it) from both East and West. Arms deals came with strings attached, sometimes openly and sometimes not. Many apparently local conflicts pitted Eastern and Western equipment and doctrine against one another, albeit in the hands of third parties. That situation changed after the collapse of the Soviet Union.

In the post-Cold War world, the arms market is far more open. It is also complicated by the emergence of new sources of equipment. Often of excellent quality, this equipment can be procured from nations in South America and Asia as well as the more traditional suppliers in Europe, North America and Russia. Chinese equipment, once notorious as knock-offs of Soviet designs, are now available on the open market as an alternative to Western equipment.

Not everything has changed, and there are still political considerations in any arms deal. Bad relations with a former supplier might result in a cut-off of spares and supplies, and interoperability with allies is always an important consideration. However, in the post-Cold War world, all kinds of military equipment are subject to a wider range of influences, and the forces of a major nation might be forced to operate in some unexpected areas.

Wars in the Gulf

The Gulf War of 1991 can be considered the first major post-Cold War conflict. Emerging from the Iran–Iraq war with an enormous military and equally huge debts to its neighbours, Iraq – under the leadership of Saddam Hussein – solved the debt problem by invading Kuwait. This negated any need to repay that nation for its loans during the Iran–Iraq war and secured

Kuwait's oil reserves as an additional source of revenue. The international response was a coalition that initially deployed forces to protect other countries neighbouring Iraq. Eventually an offensive was launched to remove Iraqi forces from Kuwait, which was accomplished despite the fact that Saddam Hussein at that time commanded the fourth-largest army in the world. However, there was no UN sanction for

Above: Soldiers of the French 21st Marine Infantry Regiment are welcomed home following a successful deployment during the Gulf War, 1991. They are wearing a three-colour, desert-sand camouflage utility uniform.

a campaign to depose Saddam Hussein, and he retained power in Iraq despite this defeat.

A second campaign was launched in 2003, this time by a much smaller coalition, to remove

Above: US troops of the Gulf War period, equipped with 'chocolate chip' desert camouflage. Even in today's high-technology battlespace there is still a need to deny an enemy rifleman an easy target.

Saddam Hussein from power. This invasion of Iraq remains controversial, but there can be no disputing that the ruling elite were extremely brutal and had used chemical weapons against rebels who opposed their rule as well as during the Iran–Iraq war. The invasion was successful, resulting in the toppling of Saddam Hussein's regime and its replacement with a democratic government. However, the process of setting up Iraq as a strong independent nation proved very difficult, not least because Iraq became a battleground where groups hating the West could attack their enemies alongside the remnants of the old regime. In this highly complex political situation, insurgents hid among the innocent people of Iraq while Western troops tried to build peace and stability. Snipers, ambushes and roadside bombs were far more common than a stand-up fight against a clear enemy. The peace in Iraq was much more hard-fought than the war.

The Era of the Three Block War

This sort of environment gives rise to terms such as 'three block war', where troops can be engaged in a firefight with insurgents, manning security checkpoints, and helping a friendly local population get their power and water supplies back online – all at the same time, and all in the space of three blocks. Terms like 'war-like situation' have entered the vocabulary in an effort to define a situation where combat is going on but there is no declared conflict or even a clear enemy.

A similar complex situation existed in Afghanistan, where the power vacuum left behind by the Soviet intervention was filled by the Taliban, a hardline fundamentalist regime that actively supported terrorism against the West. Here again, a complex situation required a mix of assertive action and patience.

After toppling the Taliban and enabling the Afghan people to install a more moderate government, Western forces had the twin objectives of building up the Afghans to the point where they could resist any resurgence on the part of the Taliban and defeating opposition to the new government. These two objectives mostly coincided, but led to additional difficulties. Many casualties were caused by infiltrators pretending to be friendly Afghan personnel, and this undermined the trust necessary between the local forces and those attempting to teach them.

This is an additional dimension in modern military operations, in which the enemy can camouflage himself among friends by wearing equipment issued to him. It has always been possible, but in situations like that in Afghanistan an infiltrator might actually be issued his 'false colours' by those he plans to betray. The purpose of uniforms was initially to enable forces to tell friend from foe, but in the modern world that can be difficult.

Contemporary Conflicts in the Middle East

At the time of writing, the main conflict ongoing in the world is in the Middle East. The rise of so-called 'Islamic State' has created a new enemy that has succeeded in capturing a significant

Turncoats

The term 'turncoat', used to describe a traitor, may have its origins in the English Civil War era, when troops turned their coats inside out to disguise themselves as members of the opposite side. This rather basic deception is said to have contributed to the capture of Corfe Castle, and there may have been occasions when defeated personnel saved themselves from capture or deliberately mingled with the enemy to obtain information.

In the modern environment, troops trying to help a nation such as Afghanistan to build an effective security apparatus run the risk of attack by turncoats who have posed as genuine recruits. These infiltrators may obtain intelligence, but have several times turned their issued weapons on their supposed allies.

expanse of territory. This is mainly in Syria and Iraq but Islamic State, or ISIL, also claims other areas including part or all of Libya, Egypt and Nigeria, and even Spain.

Opposition to ISIL is a complex business, since it is not a recognized nation and uses both conventional military and terrorist tactics. The former creates a relatively clear-cut 'war-like situation' in which targets can be attacked with airstrikes, artillery and mechanized forces that vastly outgun its militiamen. Terrorism is much harder to deal with; much of the time defence is a matter for intelligence work and preventative measures, but sometimes the terrorists can be attacked at source.

If a training camp can be identified or a leader's location obtained, a strike can be launched. This might be an airstrike or drone-launched weapons attack, but more often than not the capture or elimination of terrorists and their leaders is infantry work. Here, relatively little has changed. Personal camouflage equipment permits personnel to evade detection and slip into a defender area before carrying out a strike or calling in support.

Surgical Strikes

Even where the intent is to use air power, artillery or regular forces for a full-scale assault, observers, snipers and specialists are often positioned very close to the enemy. For example, in 2000 a group of British troops operating in Sierra Leone was taken hostage by a militia group known as the West Side Boys. A rescue mission was launched, but there was a real danger that the captives would be murdered before they could be freed.

The answer was Operation Barras, in which SAS personnel infiltrated close to the West Side Boys' camp, where they could not only report on the situation but also prevent the captives being harmed until support arrived. These personnel not only identified the position of heavy weapons, which were eliminated by attack helicopters, but kept members of the West Side Boys from approaching the British captives' position while the assault force landed from helicopters and secured the site.

The public has grown used to the idea of near-bloodless (on one side at least) 'surgical

Below: British Royal Marines deployed to Sierra Leone, wearing DPM camouflage. Note the camouflaged backpacks – to be effective, camouflage coverage must be more or less complete, without sections or objects that will draw attention.

Above: US Marine Corps from the Gulf War era wearing Desert Battle Dress Uniform (DBDU). Camouflaged versions of the NCB suit, designed to protect against chemical, biological or radioactive contamination, were used when a requirement was perceived.

strikes' of this sort, but generally has no idea how one could be performed, nor how difficult it might be. The success of an operation of this nature depends upon tight operational security and the ability of personnel to operate in close proximity to the enemy for long periods. Often, an entire operation such as Barras could be derailed by a single soldier being spotted.

The fact that several personnel can remain concealed on the fringes of a patrolled and watchful enemy camp might seem incredible if it were not done on an almost routine basis by elite forces. The difference between a successful 'surgical strike' and a chaotic bloodbath is at least in part the possession of good personal camouflage and the skills to make use of it.

Desert Camouflage

In the early 1970s, the US military began developing a desert camouflage pattern that became known as 'chocolate chip'. The primary frame of reference for this design was conditions found in the deserts of California. Initially, chocolate chip camouflage used a sandy-coloured background with irregular blobs of light and dark brown and a mix of dark and light 'rock' shapes; the nickname arose due to a resemblance to chocolate chip cookie dough.

Chocolate chip desert camouflage was produced mainly from 1981 to 1991, and was issued as Desert Battle Dress Uniform (DBDU) to personnel serving in desert environments. It was used during the 1991 Gulf War and in Somalia a little later.

Right: A British sniper wearing the desert version of Disruptive Pattern Material (DPM), Iraq, 2010. It has been suggested that the age of the Ghillie suit is over, and that 'direct action' snipers need only normal camouflage clothing like that worn by this British marksman.

However, conditions in those regions were different from the rocky Californian desert, and chocolate chip was not considered a success. As a result, a three-colour desert pattern camouflage known as DCU (Desert Camouflage Uniform) was issued beginning in 1991.

Although not appropriate to conditions in Iraq and the surrounding region, chocolate chip camouflage was adopted by several South American nations, including Argentina, Paraguay and Peru. Other nations were influenced by the original six-colour chocolate chip pattern and either copied it or based their own designs upon it. Among these are Kuwait, Iraq and Iran, suggesting that a modified chocolate chip design might have worked very well in the region.

The three-colour uniform adopted by US military personnel for desert use was based on a sandy-coloured background, with wavy horizontal lines of beige and a darker brown. Sometimes referred to as 'coffee stain' camouflage, the new uniform arrived in very small numbers in time for the 1991 Gulf War but was widely adopted thereafter. It has been copied or adapted by various other nations for use in similar conditions.

The US also experimented with 'night desert pattern' camouflage during the Gulf War. Originally developed as a possible counter to early night vision devices deployed in the Vietnam War era, this camouflage took the form of a grid pattern in dark green over a lighter background, with irregularly spaced gaps. It was issued in the form of overgarments that offered additional warmth during the cold desert night.

Unfortunately, although night desert pattern camouflage might have been useful against 1970s night vision devices it was largely ineffective against the much more advanced technology of the Gulf War era, and was withdrawn from service by the mid-1990s.

Peacekeeping and Warfighting

The Balkan conflicts of the late 1990s drew in NATO forces as well as various national and ethnic factions from the troubled region. Local forces included militia who obtained whatever equipment they could get – and were often given it by sympathetic governments or military forces. This was a 'peacekeeping' rather than 'warfighting' effort, and subject to complex rules of engagement that were mercilessly exploited by some factions.

The siege of Sarajevo is perhaps the most well-known aspect of this conflict. Surrounded and under bombardment, the defenders of Sarajevo were unable to break out but managed to hold part of the city for the better part of four years. Civilians within the city had to contend with mortar and artillery attacks as well as snipers located in high residential buildings. Notable in this conflict was the use of captured members of the peacekeeping forces as human shields against airstrikes, and the use of stolen uniforms to infiltrate peacekeeper positions. The situation for peacekeeping

troops was all but impossible, with friends, foes and innocents often hard to tell apart, and frustrating rules of engagement that often did not permit the engagement of obvious hostiles. This sort of problem has been repeated worldwide, with forces attempting to build a lasting peace coming under attack or being forced to make the difficult choice to engage or not to engage what appeared to be a real and imminent threat.

Developments in the New Millennium

The list of UN peacekeeping operations since the start of the twenty-first century is a lengthy one, with some areas appearing multiple times. Places like Côte d'Ivoire (Ivory Coast), Timor-Leste (East Timor), Burundi and Darfur have appeared in the news regularly as trouble spots, but there are many more. Personnel deployed to Indonesia, Africa and the Middle East need

Below: German troops deployed to the Balkans in 2007, wearing digital pattern camouflage.

The Modern Ghillie Suit

A suit is usually built on a top, trousers and hat, which needs enough of a 'tail' added to cover the rifle scope. Care must be taken not to overdo the amount of material incorporated into a suit. The sniper still needs to move freely, and a suit that snags on projections is as much a liability as one that fails to soften the sniper's outline sufficiently. Colour can be adjusted with spray paint, and once complete the suit is 'weathered' by generally abusing it; dragging it across concrete and dousing it in water a few times. This wears off some of the burlap and causes what is left to lie naturally. A suit can be adjusted in the field by adding scraps of foliage or removing them, subtly changing the texture and colouration of the suit.

The modern Ghillie suit is something of an art form. These British and French snipers use a common approach but the final result is a matter of personal judgement. Most Ghillie suits use a standard set of camouflage clothing as a base, with strips of burlap or jute fixed to it, using thread and/or shoe glue.

Above: This US Ranger crawls under razor-sharp barbed wire wearing a version of UCP camouflage.

different equipment for each environment, and attempts to create a universal camouflage system have not yet borne fruit.

At the same time, national armed forces have been called upon to fight wars or engage in war-like situations. Recent conflicts in Chechnya and Ukraine fall somewhere between open warfare and a peacekeeping or security operation. In such an environment, there is rarely a clear-cut 'front line' and safe rear area, and personnel whose primary role is not combat may well come under attack. Supply convoys are an obvious example, but air bases may also be attacked. Thus there is a need for the security elements of such installations to be equipped for combat operations.

In 2003, the US Air Force began testing its Airman Battle Uniform (ABU), which used a tiger-stripe pattern with a predominantly blue colouring. This was revised after testing, although the basic form of the uniform still closely resembled the BDU from which it was derived. The British RAF Regiment, which provides protection to Royal Air Force installations, is equipped with the same camouflage equipment as other British personnel.

Even naval personnel now sometimes wear camouflage uniforms. For those aboard a ship at sea, considerations other than concealment are more important. Durability, comfort and ease of movement are vital, and visibility is often an asset when many personnel are carrying out tasks in a confined area. However, camouflage may be highly useful for operations ashore. In today's world, naval personnel cannot be sure they will not see action ashore, perhaps while undertaking disaster-relief operations or when securing an installation.

The US Navy has adopted a working dress uniform similar in design to Marine Corps camouflage, but with colouration heavily biased towards blue. This is partly a matter of tradition, and partly because it hides the inevitable stains picked up when working aboard a naval vessel. Traditionally, personnel deployed ashore for combat duties or in areas where combat was possible used army-style BDUs but are currently issued camouflage uniforms similar to those used by the Marine Corps. Naval personnel attached to Marine units wear Marine camouflage.

Camouflage is now also worn by personnel not engaged in combat. Insurgents and other hostiles are not likely to make any distinction between combat troops and specialists who

are deployed for other reasons, so anyone operating in a potentially dangerous area is a possible target and given the best protection available. It has been suggested that dressing like combat forces might intimidate local populations, but the protective benefits of combat camouflage are generally considered to outweigh this factor.

Clothing the Soldier

The search for more effective equipment has never ceased, although sometimes progress is slow for budgetary or political reasons. Soldier survivability is an important consideration for many reasons. It seems only fair to provide those employed to take risks on behalf of a nation with the best protection available; in addition, morale is improved by reduced casualties, and of course the effectiveness of any military force is greater if the enemy cannot see its members properly.

Below: The US Navy has developed a BDU-style uniform, which does an excellent job of camouflaging stains that would stand out on a conventional uniform.

A properly trained sniper will rarely take more than 20–30 seconds to spot even a well-camouflaged target. However, this assumes that the sniper has a good vantage point and is not in imminent danger. For ordinary troops – whose observation skills are unlikely to be near those of a good sniper – who are taking fire and inclined to find cover, the time to spot a target and engage it may be longer than the typical rifleman is willing to stick his head up for.

A delay of even a few milliseconds in acquiring a target can give a soldier a chance to get under cover or to make a shot of his own. Obtaining those few milliseconds was one of the goals of the 'clothe the soldier' programme implemented by the Canadian government in the 1990s. Similar projects, which also included improvements in weatherproofing, durability and cooling, were carried out by other nations.

CADPAT

The Canadian armed forces were the first to receive a digital pattern camouflage uniform, known as CADPAT (CAnaDian PATtern). CADPAT is manufactured in three colour schemes: temperate woodland, arid region, and winter and arctic. It was adopted by the Canadian army in 2002 and the air force in 2004. CADPAT is also manufactured in such a way as to reduce the wearer's infrared signature and thus make detection by thermal-imaging devices less likely.

Above: Three views of a US style kevlar hemlet finished in MultiCam camouflage.

US CAMOUFLAGE

The US military issued a standardized BDU from the early 1980s, but eventually sought a replacement for various reasons. BDUs were designed to be mass-produced cheaply and were not of high quality. Similar combat uniforms, some of them copies and some actual BDUs supplied under assistance programmes, were used by various nations and some law enforcement agencies that needed camouflage clothing.

The US Marine Corps (USMC) began looking for a replacement for its BDUs at the end of the 1990s, and field testing of new uniforms began in 2001. In 2002, the USMC patented its MARPAT (MARine PATtern) camouflage system. Although imitated by other manufacturers, real MARPAT is only available to the US Marines. This is due in part to a return to the old idea of ostentation and identification. MARPAT offers good concealment in the field but when they want to be seen, US Marines also want to be readily identified as such. Like CADPAT, MARPAT incorporates measures to reduce infrared signature.

The US Army attempted to create a single camouflage pattern that would work in all terrain types, naming it Universal Camouflage Pattern (UCP). Since it is a digital pattern, UCP is also sometimes referred to as Digicam.

UPC was modelled on the Marine Corps MARPAT system but contained no black elements, on the grounds that black does not appear in nature. This approach differed from the Marine Corps and Canadian conclusions, and may not have taken into account that digital camouflage works differently from conventional or traditional methods.

Be that as it may, UCP has been criticized for not providing sufficient concealment and actually making soldiers stand out under some light conditions. As a result, in 2014 the US Army adopted a new Operational Camouflage Pattern (OCP) designated Scorpion W2.

Previous attempts to replace the traditional BDUs included the issue of MultiCam, a seven-colour system originally adopted by the US Army in 2002 but displaced by UCP in 2004. MultiCam attracted renewed interest at the end of the decade, when it was designated Operation Enduring Freedom camouflage pattern (OEFCP). The use of a specific operational name as a designator suggests that its adoption may have been considered a temporary measure.

MultiCam has also been used by some law enforcement agencies and is on sale to the public. Some nations do not permit the wearing of camouflage clothing by non-military personnel under any circumstances – in some

Opposite: This US Marine wears the woodland pattern MARPAT camouflage and has painted his face to obscure recognition and reflection.

Right: A soldier from the US 10th Mountain Division during the campaign in Afghanistan, 2010. The Universal Camouflage Pattern (UCP) was an attempt to create a one-size-hides-all camouflage system. However, performance in tropical and forested terrain was not as good as had been hoped for, and other camouflage systems have now replaced UCP.

Above: This US Navy SEAL sniper has added strands of local vegetation to his personal camouflage, breaking up the distinctive shapes of his rifle barrel, scope and head.

cases it is a criminal offence – while others restrict only patterns on current issue to serving personnel. In other cases, such as MARPAT, sale of camouflage items can be restricted by patent law. However, designs such as MultiCam are available for use by hunters and by those who find camouflage fashionable.

BRITISH CAMOUFLAGE

The British Army used Disruptive Pattern Material (DPM) for many years, with new versions appearing as part of projects such as Pattern 1994 DPM, Soldier 95 and Soldier 2000. Eventually, DPM was replaced with a variant of MultiCam designated Multi-Terrain Pattern (MTP). British MTP uses designs similar to DPM but in a MultiCam colouration. The Australian armed forces also issued its own variant for personnel serving in Afghanistan.

CHINESE CAMOUFLAGE

Chinese forces made limited use of camouflage material from the 1970s onwards, with early patterns resembling British DPM. Initially issued only to elite forces, camouflage became more common over time. Early equipment was replaced with a reversible version, with a DPM-like pattern on one side and a duck-hunter scheme on the other. Experimentation went on, with schemes resembling NATO woodland camouflage entering service in the 1980s and a bluish pattern for marines appearing in 1990.

Between 1990 and 2007, when pixellated patterns began to appear, Chinese forces received limited issue of a range of camouflage schemes. A desert pattern similar to contemporary US designs was used for a time by special forces units, and an urban scheme was sighted during parades. It is not clear whether this was ever intended for use in the field, however. A variant of the German Flecktarn system was also used for operations in Tibet.

From 2007, pixellated camouflage began to be issued as a universal design, although colour

Below: CADPAT (CAnaDian PATtern) was the first digital-pattern camouflage system issued to any armed force. It also included thermal-emission reduction measures.

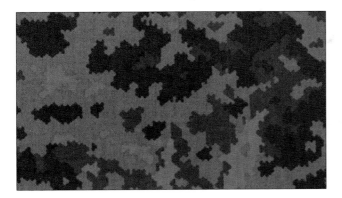

Below: Tropentarn is the German armed forces' desert camouflage pattern. It uses a three-colour system with brown and green on a tan background.

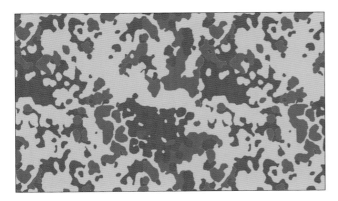

Below: The M05 system is used by the Finnish armed forces. Depicted is the woodland variant; arctic, desert and urban versions also exist.

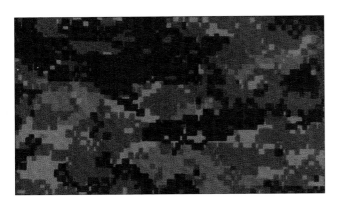

Below: DPM, or Disruptive Pattern Material, was used by British armed forces by many years. It is no longer officially in use, but may see deployment in jungle terrain.

Below: MTP, or Multi-Terrain Pattern, was adopted by the British Army in 2010. The pattern has been designed to resemble the DPM pattern, so it looks distinctively British.

Below: MultiCam was developed for the US Army but quickly supplanted by the Universal Camouflage Pattern, before being reinstated in 2010.

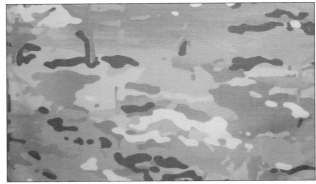

schemes varied according to terrain. This pattern was issued to air force units in a blue and grey colouration, with mountain, tropical, woodland and 'oceanic' versions also in service. Other designs, including what appears to be a version of MultiCam, have also been seen on Chinese military personnel.

Urban Environments Today

All modern militaries must consider the need to operate in urban environments, and this has imposed new requirements upon camouflage development. Many police and law enforcement agencies operate paramilitary elements such as hostage-rescue teams, and there is a move towards camouflage for these personnel.

Although there is much to say for the impressiveness and intimidation factor of black-clad police moving up to deal with a hostage situation, concealment and surprise are also recognized as highly useful. For this reason, some police agencies have begun to experiment with urban camouflage, as have a number of military forces. Since engagement ranges in urban combat tend to be relatively short, urban camouflage designs need to use smaller patterns

Below: China has undertaken considerable investment in digital camouflage systems. Variants of the Type 07 camouflage exist to match most common terrain types. The pattern consists of mid-brown, grey-green and small elements of very dark green on a neutral grey background.

Above: These US Army Rangers, on exercise in 2007, are wearing MultiCam camouflage. Variants are now produced for snow, desert, tropical and urban terrain.

that must also incorporate more vertical and horizontal elements to fit with the background.

Even so, concealment can be difficult – not least because the colour of urban and suburban areas can vary enormously. Concrete and similar grey backgrounds are common, but so are small grassy or bushy areas and backdrops of brick or wood. Digital camouflage that breaks up the distinctive shape of the human body while blending with at least some background colours is useful, but so is camouflage that makes it difficult to target the wearer effectively.

Camouflage systems such as Tactical Assault Camouflage (TACAM) may offer counterterrorism personnel advantages in urban terrain, and militaries worldwide have also attempted to produce urban-oriented personal camouflage. One example was the experimental US dual-texture system developed but not implemented in the 1970s for use in what is now known as military operations in urban terrain

(MOUT). A later but similar concept, named simply 'urban camouflage' but sometimes called T-MOUT, was also not adopted.

One reason for this is the difficulty in creating an effective urban camouflage pattern, but there is also the factor that urban terrain offers so many opportunities for concealment that do not rely upon personal camouflage. Lessons learned in the 'rattenkreig' of the Battle of Stalingrad still apply today; movement within buildings and other structures, or behind solid walls, offers near-complete concealment. This is not the case when outside cities, so if only one form of camouflage can be worn, one that matches the natural environment is likely to be much more generally useful than one that is optimized for urban terrain.

CHAPTER 3

CAMOUFLAGE IN LAND WARFARE

Buildings and vehicles have numerous straight lines and areas of shadow that can give away their identity. Blending such an object into a natural background poses unique challenges.

At the outbreak of the Great War, a solid front line was also a defence against enemy information gathering and reconnaissance. It was possible to sneak into an enemy trench at night to grab a prisoner, and in more fluid situations, cavalry might penetrate some distance into enemy territory and return with useful information. However, for the most part the very existence of a 'front line' made it difficult for the enemy to see what lay beyond it.

Close to the front, a traditional style of camouflage was required. Observation posts were necessary to monitor the enemy's trench lines and were subject to harassment from enemy artillery as well as snipers and machine

guns. Even if he were not hit, an observer in an elevated and vulnerable position was unlikely to produce good information if he were under constant fire. Concealing these positions was thus essential to their survival and effective operation.

Many observation posts were located on hills, up trees or on the upper floors of ruined buildings. Likely points were obvious to an enemy who had become trench-crafty, but might be left alone if it was not known they were currently in use. The precise location of an observation post could be concealed by camouflaging it, while the fact that it was in use was hidden by entering stealthily under cover of darkness.

All of this effort could be undone by observers who gave away their position, so personnel had to learn what amounted to a concealment doctrine. The guidelines that emerged were based on common sense and observation of consequences in a wholly

Opposite: Experience in World War II showed that a simple application of irregular white or off-white blotches to an armoured vehicle provided effective camouflage in winter conditions. As recently as the NATO deployment in the Balkans, this quick-and simple method has proven highly useful, even though more technological options now exist.

Above: A German observation post during World War I. The more or less static nature of trench warfare made such positions a useful prospect. However, they were by their very nature rather hazardous to use unless concealed in some manner.

unforgiving environment, and were not complex. Limiting movement, not showing lights and being patient were vital to the survival of the post and its observers. Cool nerves were necessary when entering and leaving a position; hasty movement could attract attention and, soon afterwards, gunfire.

Deep reconnaissance was virtually unknown at the outbreak of the Great War. Even before the war stagnated into solid trench lines there was a limit to how far cavalry – traditionally the primary source of reconnaissance on enemy

dispositions – could penetrate. Once the Western Front became what was essentially a gigantic siege, reconnaissance on the ground was limited to what could be seen from an elevated position or learned by a raiding party sneaking across no-man's land at night.

Camouflage and Concealment

Camouflage and concealment still played a role in warfare of this era and before. During the American Civil War, many artillery batteries covering strategically important rivers were camouflaged, and on land batteries could be concealed by terrain or by infantry positioned in front of the battery.

Such a 'masked battery' features in many accounts of clever stratagems from the era, not all of which were particularly accurate. The sudden fire of artillery from an unexpected direction could rout a unit or inflict heavy casualties if the enemy advanced deep into its field of fire; a commander who could contrive this would rightly be seen as a tactical expert. This was difficult to achieve, however, and most accounts seem to have originated in the imagination of newspapermen.

That is not to say that the concept was not part of the doctrine of the time. Officer cadets at West Point and Sandhurst were taught that batteries should be concealed 'by some contrivance' until called upon to fire, and at least some of the accounts of their use during the American Civil War and similar conflicts are reliable.

The concept of the artillery battery masked by some form of concealment is entirely workable, although it depended upon the enemy moving in a predictable manner. The artillery of the late nineteenth century had a short effective range and could achieve decisive results against infantry only at very short distances. Canister

Above: Reports of actions in the American Civil War include many references to masked batteries, some of which are accurate. Both sides constructed concealed artillery positions to control rivers, ambushing enemy gunboats as they passed.

and grapeshot were fearsome man-killers close in, but the rifles of the era could easily hit an artillery crew at this range.

Thus, the masked battery had a very short engagement window within which to break infantry in front of it. A slugging match with infantry who had dispersed into a skirmish line was a losing prospect for most artillery crews. Nevertheless, the idea of a concealed artillery battery as the decisive stroke of a battle passed into the popular imagination; it even features in science fiction. In H.G. Wells' *The War of the Worlds* (1898), one of the few successes scored against the Martians is won by a masked gun battery, opening fire on an unsuspecting Fighting Machine from close range with great effect.

This required a countermeasure. Digging artillery into defensive positions that would protect against a near miss offered a degree of defence, but the sheer volume of fire that could

Inspirations for New Technologies

H.G. Wells was writing at a time when warfare was changing rapidly. In *The War of the Worlds,* humans gain the secret of powered flight, which they had not yet attained, from the wrecks of Martian flyers. Not many years after Wells published his book, human flight became a reality. This opened up a whole new dimension, with reconnaissance aircraft able to fly deep into enemy territory and report on or even photograph enemy positions. Using a map and data from aerial reconnaissance, artillery – which had recently gained greatly extended ranges – could strike with reasonable accuracy at points well behind enemy lines. Artillery positions, supply dumps and concentration areas could be shelled by gunners who would never see them.

Flight and photography proved an effective combination during World War I. Denying the enemy the benefits of aerial reconnaissance soon emerged as a key mission.

Above: It is not always possible to completely hide something as large as a building, but it may be possible to make it look like something innocuous. In this case, a British brigade headquarters has been disguised as a haystack to deceive aerial reconnaissance.

be delivered made counterbattery fire a deadly threat. Moving gun positions was laborious and only effective for a short time before the reconnaissance aircraft found them again. But what if aerial observers could not find the gun positions at all?

The answer, of course, was to camouflage them. This was a new concept at the time, with no established concepts or guidelines. There was no body of knowledge on what the ground looks like from the air; no ready reference on what could be easily recognised and what could not. Shadows fall differently when seen from the air, and camouflage that seemed effective from the ground might be

obvious from above. Thus, the early camoufleurs had to feel their way and develop concepts based on observation and guesswork.

Not surprisingly, many of the early camoufleurs were painters, who understood colour and shadow and could apply this knowledge to their new line of work. However, all they could do was take an educated guess and try out the results. How much feedback was available from friendly reconnaissance pilots remains open to debate; aircraft were not available in large numbers at the beginning of the Great War and their commanders were not always receptive to launching sorties to see what their own side was doing.

However, the science of camouflaging artillery positions from aerial observation advanced quite rapidly. Camoufleurs tried out a wide range of schemes and patterns, and even created camouflage in the styles of various great master painters to see which offered the best protection at different distances.

Armoured Fighting Vehicles

The value of surprise in warfare is well understood. As previously noted, the sudden intense fire of the masked battery could be decisive, but there are other forms of surprise. Among them is what can be termed 'technological surprise', which occurs when one side fields a weapon or capability for which the other is unprepared. The arrival of the armoured fighting vehicle on the battlefield was one such example of technological surprise.

The development of the armoured fighting vehicle by the Western Allies was not a total

shock to the Central Powers, of course. Various concepts for a mobile armoured combat platform had been put forward in the years of the Great War, and science fiction novels had been written about them. Armoured cars were in use on both sides; some of them quite well protected. Nevertheless, the deployment of what would come to be known as 'tanks' by the Allies was unnerving to the soldiers who faced them, and few effective countermeasures were available.

One reason for this was the strict security around the programme, which resulted in armoured vehicles being known to this day as 'tanks'. It was considered inevitable that objects so big would be spotted and reported on, so a cover story was created that they were mobile water reservoirs. This sort of informational camouflage has been used many times before and since, but rarely has it had such a permanent effect.

By creating a plausible explanation for what the objects might be, the Allies managed to

Below: Although the appearance of armoured fighting vehicles was a terrifying shock to the troops facing them, this surprise was largely wasted by a poor choice of initial deployment. Even on the much better terrain at Cambrai many tanks became stuck in ditches and shell holes.

Above: The French Renault FT17 tank was developed with the needs of trench warfare in mind, but ended up serving right through the 1920s and 1930s, by which time it was totally obsolete. Many examples were given camouflage paint that was reasonably effective at long ranges, but virtually useless close up.

deflect deeper investigation. The vehicles were also moved to the front in great secrecy and kept under cover during the day. All aspects of the deployment of these potentially decisive weapons were protected by camouflage and deception; the vehicles themselves, their location, and even their nature were all closely guarded secrets.

In the event, tanks did not turn out to be the war-winning weapon that had been hoped for. The ground chosen for their initial deployment was unsuitable and their technical limitations resulted in many breakdowns. Yet the few tanks that engaged the enemy caused great alarm and, in some cases, rout. Apparently impervious to gunfire, a lone tank cleared a village of German defenders, with the British infantry reportedly 'cheering along behind'.

The troops fleeing from this first tank attack were not lacking in courage. However, they were faced with something new and unknown, which seemed unstoppable and deadly. Thus, the tank combined two great fears: the unknown and the overwhelming enemy. Later tank attacks produced greater results, but the shock that a massed first tank attack over suitable ground might have caused was never realized.

By the time the famous large-scale tank assault was launched at Cambrai in 1917, the German infantry knew what they were facing and had countermeasures available. The armour-piercing rifle bullets they were hastily issued were ineffective against the improved Mk IV tanks used at Cambrai, but they bolstered morale. Bundles of grenades and improvised antitank guns – actually light artillery pieces – offered an effective defence.

Camouflage also played a part in defence against tank attack. Concealed ditches and 'tank traps' could immobilize a tank, while concealed artillery pieces positioned to fire directly on the advancing tanks – effectively masked batteries making a reappearance on the battlefield – were the most potent tank-killers of the day.

By the time of Cambrai, tanks were fearsome but no longer unknown. They could be destroyed, and the defenders knew it. Camouflage on a grand scale had given the tank a great opportunity, but poor tactical choices largely wasted that opportunity. Camouflaged guns and determined infantry who waited in concealment to attack the tank with explosives proved an effective countermeasure. A tank's guns could destroy these batteries; machine guns could cut down infantry who attempted a close assault. However, the crew had very limited visibility and could be caught by surprise, turning a tank assault into an ambush.

Armoured Vehicle Camouflage

The first tanks were camouflaged before going into action, but were never intended to conceal themselves when in proximity to the enemy. Huge, high-sided monstrosities, they were too obvious to conceal when on the move. This did not preclude concealment before an attack or a counterattack; one idea put forward was for tanks to be concealed along the defensive line in small numbers or even alone, emerging like 'savage rabbits' from their places of concealment to launch an immediate and powerful counterattack in the case of an enemy breakthrough.

The 'savage rabbits' concept was never realized, but the idea that a concealed tank could inflict a terrifying reverse upon an enemy who thought he was succeeding was borne out in later conflicts. In the meantime, armoured vehicles were quickly proven to be anything but impervious to enemy fire. A range of weapons was deployed against them with varying degrees of effectiveness. Bundles of grenades, magnetic mines, satchel charges, antitank rifles and armour-piercing bullets were given to the infantry, eventually followed by man-portable antitank weapons.

However, the main threat to tanks came from antitank guns, whether emplaced or mounted on another tank. The latter did not occur quickly; most tanks of the inter-war years were designed for infantry support rather than to fight other armoured vehicles and were armed with weapons poorly suited to penetrating armour. This was remedied in the early part of World War II, and soon a vast array of antitank weaponry had reached the battlefield. Among these weapons were tank destroyers; essentially turretless tanks whose main gun had a very

Aerial Photo-reconnaissance

Camouflaging vehicles and positions against aerial observation became ever more of a challenge during World War II. Photo-reconnaissance with the primitive cameras of World War I era produced low-quality images, making it hard to discern even objects that were not well camouflaged. By the end of the 1930s, far more effective equipment was available and could be carried much deeper into enemy territory. With more and better photographs to work from, the photo-analysts were far harder to deceive. In the tactical sense, the problem was not so severe. Faster-flying aircraft provided the pilot with less time to spot and identify a target. Camouflage only had to impose a slight delay in this process to protect its users, and similarly even a slight increase in the difficulty of aiming an airborne weapon could be life-saving. Thus for vehicles on the move even the most basic of camouflage measures were worth taking.

limited field of traverse. The low silhouette of a tank destroyer made it a difficult target.

Camouflage played an important part in antitank warfare. Throughout the war, antitank positions were found to be most effective if they were not discovered until they opened fire – the concept of the masked battery again. This also applied to tanks operating in this role. Mobile-tank-versus-tank battles did occur, but shooting on the move was inaccurate; firing from a concealed position at an unsuspecting enemy's flank was preferable.

Vehicle Camouflage in World War II

After the Normandy invasion of 1944, the Allies were forced to advance through the Bocage, a region characterized by thick hedgerows and poor long-distance visibility. This 'hedgerow hell' was ideal for ambushes by tanks and infantry, with quite small numbers of tanks or antitank guns holding up the Allied advance or inflicting serious casualties.

In addition to ambushes by guns and other armoured vehicles, World War II tanks faced a threat that their predecessors had not – air power that was capable of destroying armoured vehicles. Rockets were a popular antitank weapon, though 'tankbuster' aircraft were fielded by both sides. These were equipped with a relatively heavy gun – sometimes more than one – carried under the wings or fuselage. Conventional bombs could also be used.

Stationary tanks, such as those refuelling or marshalling for an attack, were vulnerable to artillery or air attack, but those on the move were not immune to the tankbusters. Although high speed could make a tank hard to hit, camouflage was highly useful in defeating these attacks. Elaborate concealment was possible for a refuelling or rearming depot, or for an ambush position, but even rudimentary camouflage was useful against air attack.

A pilot crossing the battlefield looking for a target had at best a few seconds to spot a promising target, identify it as an enemy unit, and line up an attack. Even a small margin of error in his aim could render the attack ineffective. Tanks that moved cautiously, using hedges and other terrain features for cover, might escape notice or might not present a good enough target to draw a pilot's attention.

Soviet commanders implemented a practice of moving tanks in single file to conceal their numbers even when they were not following a road. A single set of tracks might be spotted by

reconnaissance aircraft, but it was not possible to determine how many tanks had passed. Halts were made in woods or under cover, and wires were sometimes used to pull trees together over a road to conceal vehicles using it or halted upon it.

In addition to denying the enemy accurate reconnaissance data and making a unit as a whole more difficult to attack, a more personal factor was at play here, too. Pilots would generally pick the easiest target, so a camouflaged tank using cover was less likely to be attacked than another member of the same unit that was moving more openly. Camouflage and the use of concealment was thus useful from a personal survival point of view even if another tank in the same unit was successfully attacked.

Below: With their limited traverse guns and low silhouette, tank destroyers like this M-10 pictured during the Ardennes Offensive were best suited to an ambush role.

GERMAN ARMY VEHICLE CAMOUFLAGE

The German army used vehicle camouflage, but did not set out standard patterns. Instead, instructions were issued spelling out the colours to be used, with general guidelines on how to apply them. In the early part of the war, most vehicles were coloured all-over *dunkelgrau* (dark grey), with some having additional brown camouflage. This *dunkelgrau* provided quite good concealment at a distance, with the vehicle tending to fade into the horizon, but was rather more obvious at closer ranges.

The first German armoured vehicles sent to North Africa wore *dunkelgrau*, and were very obvious against the light sandy backdrop. Various expedients were applied in the field, until later in 1941 *gelbbraun* (tan) paint was officially supplied. By mid-1942, paint shortages caused further expedients to be attempted. The result was

Above: Festoons of branches break up the blocky outline of this Tiger tank photographed during the Normandy campaign. It is not possible to camouflage the front of the tank in this manner without impeding crew vision.

typically a two-tone grey and brown camouflage pattern, the exact details of which varied.

Experience in winter conditions also caused the German army to quickly find ways to camouflage its grey vehicles. *Dunkelgrau* stood out too much against snow, but an irregular application of whitewash created effective camouflage. Other expedients included draping the vehicle in sheets or any other light-coloured cloth that could be obtained.

As the war went on and the situation deteriorated, it was not uncommon for units intended for one theatre to be diverted to another, arriving with entirely the wrong camouflage on its vehicles. To counter this, from some time in 1943 onwards, all German armoured vehicles were given a base colour named *dunkelgelb*. This translates as 'dark yellow', although the shade could vary considerably depending upon where the paint was manufactured and how much it had aged.

Dunkelgelb was the base colour for a camouflage scheme known as *Hinterhalt-tarnung*

Below: An early-war Panzer II wearing a uniform *dunkelgrau* (top) contrasted with a Panzer IV wearing one of the many camouflage patterns based on *dunkelgelb*. This *dunkelgrau* colour scheme looked impressive and offered some concealment advantages at a distance, but was very obvious in some terrain types.

(ambush pattern). The name of this camouflage scheme reflects the tactics of the era; German armoured units were adept at ambushing enemy forces from concealment, thus reducing the advantage of numbers possessed by their opponents. In September 1944, German practice changed again, with the *dunkelgelb* base coat omitted and camouflage applied over red oxide primer. It has been suggested that this was done due to a shortage of material to make *dunkelgelb* paint, or perhaps in recognition that the Axis' armoured forces were now fighting in different terrain conditions as the Allies advanced.

Ambush pattern was reimposed a few weeks later, at least in theory – like later camouflage orders, this could not be implemented on a

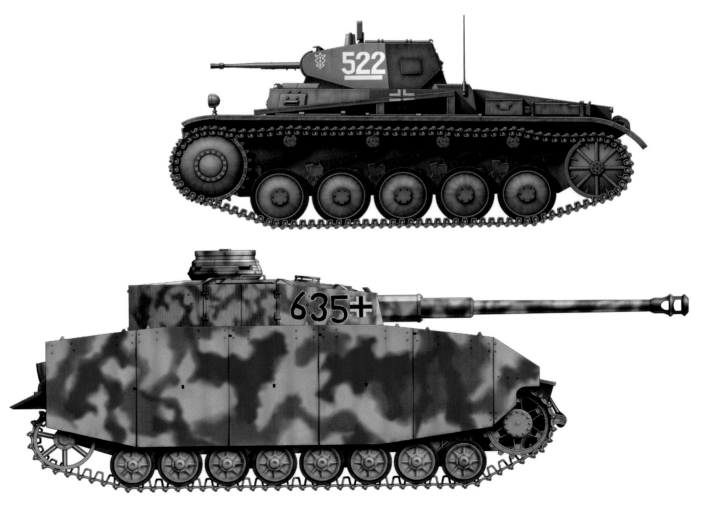

Left: A British Cromwell tank in basic olive green, contrasted with a Cruiser MkII (A10) tank in one of many desert colour schemes. The blue stripe is the result of attempting to approximate the designated disruptive colour scheme, which used a silver-grey that was often not available.

uniform basis. Towards the end of the war, German vehicles were camouflaged with whatever paint and materials were available. Units on all sides made extensive use of natural cover as well as nets and tarpaulins, but – officially or otherwise – German forces took this a step further. It was not uncommon for a unit retreating ahead of its fellows to prepare supplies of ready-cut foliage and branches, as well as scavenged materials, to be left behind for the following formations. This enabled a new concealed position to be set up quickly when the unit stopped to fight.

BRITISH ARMY VEHICLE CAMOUFLAGE

As with the German army, the British armoured forces began the war with vehicles painted in a single colour. In the British case, this was a dark green that could appear black in poor

light. Disruptive patterns of light and dark green began to appear in 1939, with camouflage patterns being modified in 1941–42 due to a lack of critical materials.

During 1942–44, the primary concern was to conceal tanks from aerial reconnaissance and attack, resulting in a variety of patterns in green and brown. From April 1944, olive drab became the standard base colour, largely because many vehicles were supplied by the USA and were already painted that colour. Disruptive patterns were abandoned under an Army Council Instruction issued in April 1944.

In the Middle East, a pale cream colour was used before the war, with sand and stone colours substituted from July 1939. Pale cream reappeared with the arrival of many new vehicles in 1940, and was often used as the base for camouflage schemes such as the three-colour

Caunter scheme. This was replaced at the end of 1941 by a simple light stone colouration, sometimes with an additional colour to create a disruptive pattern. Black and white were both used to create a disruptive contrast.

Further modifications occurred later, with desert pink and various shades of green and brown being added to the colour mix available in October 1942. There were considerable local variations and many exceptions to the official desert camouflage schemes, some of which occurred because of a shortage of the correct materials or the leisure to alter camouflage to meet official guidelines.

SOVIET VEHICLE CAMOUFLAGE

Although the Soviet authorities began experimenting with armoured vehicle camouflage in 1939, the Axis invasion of Russian began before measures could be properly implemented. Many Soviet units implemented their own camouflage systems at the outbreak of war, using whatever materials they could obtain and inventing designs that seemed potentially useful.

Most vehicles at this time were painted olive drab. A system of green, yellow-earth and dark brown was proposed to replace this, to be applied in specified proportions. The new camouflage colour guidance came with instructions on

how to paint a vehicle or artillery piece in order to disguise its outline. Soviet camouflage instructions mentioned that stencils should not be used for camouflage shapes, in order to prevent them from being too regular.

It is notable that Soviet artillery was often camouflaged even when tanks were not, presumably since vehicles could move around more to evade detection and air attack whereas the relatively static artillery relied more upon concealment. The three-colour scheme was considered to give the best disruptive effect, although in practice applications could vary considerably.

White was used for winter camouflage, sometimes by simply painting a tank white all over and sometimes in patches over other colours. Many winter patterns were unofficial, and were based upon the observations of tank crews themselves. The use of foliage and other camouflage materials was likewise often governed by rules of thumb and guesswork rather than a central doctrine.

Right: A Soviet T-34 wearing winter camouflage created by using a thin whitewash over its base colour.

Soviet Vehicle Camouflage Compared

The tanks of the Red Army fought in terrain that changed considerably between summer and winter, and camouflage techniques advanced as a result of harsh experience, first against Finland and later Germany.

T-26 Model 1938 Light Tank

This pre-war T-26 wears a three-tone summer camouflage scheme. The Red Army used a dark green base, and individual tank crews would then add shades of brown to create a pattern.

BT-5 Fast Tank

The BT-5TU is a command variant of the successful BT design. This example wears olive/off-white winter camouflage.

KV-1 Model 1940 Heavy Tank

The heavy KV-1 tank was extremely tough but still benefited from concealment. This example wears three-tone summer camouflage.

SU-122 Assault Gun

The SU-122 assault gun was built on the chassis of the T-34 tank. This example wears white winter camouflage garnished with foliage patterns.

ISU-152 Self-propelled Gun

The ISU-152 self-propelled gun could function as a heavy tank destroyer when needed. This example wears late-war four-tone summer camouflage.

Operation Bertram:
False Armies in the Desert

The war in North Africa was critical to the conflict elsewhere. An Axis victory would deprive the Allies of the Suez Canal and grant their opponents access to the oil fields of the Middle East. At the same time, it was a drain on Axis manpower and equipment that was needed elsewhere. The balance tipped one way then the other, with Axis forces under General Erwin Rommel eventually halted by strong Allied positions at El Alamein.

Both sides needed to break the deadlock, but were funnelled into a narrow coastal strip by the impassable Qattara Depression to the south. The Axis army, now at the end of a long supply line, had to break through or retreat – and Rommel was not one to take that option. Correctly predicting that the main Axis attack would come in the south of the defensive line, newly appointed Allied commander Bernard Montgomery placed his defences to defeat it.

Above: The opposite of camouflage in many ways, this dummy Sherman is lifelike enough to fool a reconnaissance pilot at a reasonable distance.

Having prevented the Axis breakthrough, Montgomery needed to advance. He faced strong positions backed by mobile reserves, which would be difficult if not impossible to break through. Heavy casualties seemed inevitable either way. To even the odds, Montgomery set about implementing one of the most elaborate deception operations in history.

Code-named Operation Bertram, the deception used all possible avenues. False radio signals were sent to suggest that the Allies were deploying for a major offensive in the south. This was corroborated by the construction of a fake pipeline, ostensibly to bring up fuel for the attack. The pipeline was constructed with apparent determination but rather slowly, creating the impression that the attack was scheduled for later than the actual intent.

Above: The enormous deception effort undertaken at El Alamein included measures to make trucks look like tanks, and – as depicted here – tanks look like trucks. The upper structure was entirely sufficient to fool enemy reconnaissance pilots glimpsing distant vehicles into believing they were seeing a supply convoy.

in the north were merely decoys, Axis commanders were further convinced that the real attack was coming in the south. Shortly before the attack was to be made, these dummy positions were replaced with real weapons.

Concealment and deception played a critical role in the success of Operation Bertram. A canopy referred to as a 'sunshield' was constructed over the top of tanks, making them look like supply trucks from the air. A similar apparatus, resembling a tank's upper surfaces and turret and placed atop a light vehicle, was used to create mobile dummy tanks. Artillery pieces and their towing vehicles were concealed inside fake trucks known as 'cannibals'.

At the same time, the main armoured forces were positioned well behind the defensive line; nowhere near close enough to launch an offensive. The enemy was allowed to see these real tanks and the trucks that were positioned close to the projected jumping-off point for the operation until two days before the commencement of the attack, when the tanks were brought up to their ready positions. With the tanks disguised with sunshield canopies and the trucks now in the rear disguised as tanks, it looked to the enemy as if nothing had changed.

Supplies for the offensive were also disguised as trucks, with piles of ration and ammunition boxes constructed to match the general

The southern pipeline would not have deceived anyone if it had not led to a dummy depot where an apparently large number of armoured vehicles were staging for the attack. Some of the units assigned to the area were real, but large numbers of dummies were created to give the impression of a powerful force.

At the same time, a complex double bluff was carried out in the north. More dummy forces were created, including tanks and artillery positions, which were intended to be initially convincing. However, as the date of the attack neared, these dummies were increasingly neglected until their true nature became obvious. Now aware that some of the forces facing them

Above: Dummy aircraft were used tactically, to divert fire from real ones when an airfield was attacked, and in a strategic sense to mislead the enemy about the strength and location of Allied air power. From the air this dummy Hurricane looks entirely convincing.

shape of a truck as seen from the air and then camouflaged to complete the deception. Fuel was hidden in cans that lined trenches. None of this would have worked if the enemy had been able to undertake detailed air reconnaissance, but Allied air superiority was sufficient to exclude almost all Axis planes from the region. Those that did manage to make a reconnaissance saw what the Allied camoufleurs wanted them to, and reported it to their commanders.

The deception was assisted by the enemy's preconceptions. In front of the Axis positions in the north lay a wide belt of minefields that would cause heavy casualties among tanks. Approaching by this route seemed undesirable for that reason,

False Guns

A protective measure applied to some tanks was the false gun carried by many command tanks. Removing the armament created more room inside the vehicle for a map table and radio equipment, but the lack of a barrel protruding from the turret would mark the vehicles as a command unit and therefore a high-value target. A false gun took up no room inside but enabled the command tank to blend in with others in its unit, with the result that it would draw no more fire than any other vehicle. This principle was no different to the practice of concealing rank insignia and carrying a rifle followed by some infantry officers. The officer remained a target, but a less attractive one.

Left: A dummy aircraft did not have to be particularly elaborate – fabric draped over a frame would work well enough. However, shadows (or the lack of them) would give away the deception for what it was, so the dummy had to be at roughly the right height.

further strengthening the belief that the main attack would come in the south. However, Montgomery had planned for this. Rather than armour leading the assault – as was conventional at that time – the attack would initially be made by infantry, who would not set off antitank mines. Engineers would follow them to clear lanes in the minefield, and the armour could then move up in support.

This strategy was a gamble, relying as it did on the enemy reacting as planned. In the event, the Axis commanders were completely deceived and were convinced that the Allies had a greater force available than was actually the case. Surprise was total when the 'fake' guns opened fire, and the assault on Rommel's position was ultimately a success.

However, the Allies did not have it all their own way. Even with the enemy badly out of position and caught unawares, the breakthrough was difficult to achieve. Nevertheless, once the Axis forces were dislodged from their positions facing El Alamein, they were driven back all the way to Tunisia and ultimately out of Africa.

Operation Quicksilver: A Fictional Invasion Force

By 1944, the Allies were finally in a position to attempt a landing in northern Europe. This was a

difficult proposition: the enemy knew they were coming, and the choice of landing areas was not extensive. The buildup of forces for the invasion was hard to miss. However, it might be possible to delay the commitment of enemy reserves if doubt could be created about the intended landing area.

Complex deception plans were implemented under the collective heading of Operation Bodyguard. This incorporated many elements, some of them very far from northern Europe, but the most important was a plan to reinforce the Axis leaders' predisposition to expect an invasion across the Straits of Dover. This was the shortest route, reducing time at sea, and permitted aircraft to remain over the invasion area for the longest possible duration.

It is always easier to convince an enemy that his preconceived ideas are correct than to change his mind, and since it was known that Hitler and his staff believed an invasion would come across the Pas de Calais then deception operations were aimed at ensuring this idea remained fixed in their minds. A successful deception operation named Fortitude North did convince the Axis to move more troops into Norway in order to prevent an Allied landing there, but the main theatre was the Channel coast, where Operation Fortitude South was being implemented.

Fortitude South incorporated a number of elements. Air reconnaissance was concentrated on the Pas de Calais area to reinforce the conviction that the Allies intended to land there, while an entire fake army group was created along with supporting infrastructure. This was codenamed Quicksilver, and was commanded by General George Patton. Patton was a logical choice for leader of a major offensive; his appointment further reinforced the conviction that the blow would fall around Calais.

Extensive electronic deception was carried out in the form of false radio traffic between elements of the fictitious army, but to be convincing this had to be backed up by physical means. Huge numbers of inflatable tanks and trucks were deployed to create the illusion that Patton's imaginary First United States Army Group (FUSAG) was the actual invasion force. These would be carried by equally false landing craft made from plywood. Great care had to be taken to prevent these lightweight dummies from blowing around in a stiff breeze and revealing the

deception, and of course the whole force had to be camouflaged just not quite well enough to be spotted but to be convincing.

Infrastructure in the form of fake airfields and fuel depots were also created; again, these had to be not quite concealed if they were to be convincing to the enemy. The camoufleurs who constructed and disguised these decoys required a high level of understanding of their craft in order to create the illusion that enemy reconnaissance pilots had seen something they were not intended to.

Ultimately, Operation Bodyguard was an enormous success. Three weeks after the landings

Below: Dummy landing craft were constructed from plywood, and inflatable dummies were also deployed. The key threat to this deception was the way the boats moved, especially in a choppy sea. Landing craft bouncing around on the end of a rope were not likely to be very convincing.

The Canal Defence Light

Some concealment methods were unconventional. The Canal Defence Light was mounted on a tank chassis and used to illuminate a target during night attacks or to blind defenders and make their return fire ineffective. Even if the light were not aimed directly at defenders, its brilliance could ruin their night vision and make it difficult to distinguish any target other than the light-equipped tank. The vehicle would draw fire but was armoured, whereas the troops its light helped conceal were not. The Canal Defence Light arrived too late in the war to have much impact, especially since the secrecy surrounding it meant that many commanders never heard about it and therefore did not use it. However, it was useful at the Rhine crossings in the last days of the war.

Above: The Canal Defence Light provided concealment by tricking the eye with areas of bright illumination and darkness.

in Normandy, German forces that might have made a counterattack were still being held in reserve to counter the expected landings by FUSAG. The intervention of these forces might have been decisive, but by the time they were committed it was far too late.

Blinds, Decoys and Dummies

Decoys were also used on a much smaller scale during World War II. A single sniper was often enough to hold up an advance for some time, or to inflict numerous casualties before he was eliminated. Various methods were used to make snipers reveal themselves, many of them crude. The trick of holding up a helmet or supporting one on a rifle barrel in the hope of convincing a sniper that an unwise infantryman had stuck his head up could sometimes work, but it was an obvious gambit and unlikely to fool a skilled sniper.

Some units created much more convincing dummies to try to draw sniper fire. The most elaborate included weapons that could be aimed and fired by pulling on wires. There was no chance of actually hitting anything with such a weapon, but gunfire might serve to convince a sniper or a group of troublesome well-concealed enemy infantrymen that the dummy was real. If a sniper was shooting at a dummy some distance from an infantry position, he was not targeting those who were looking for him and might give away his position.

Some personnel used inventive means to create ready-made camouflaged positions. One such measure was a simple umbrella, painted to match the local vegetation.

This was easy to carry but could be positioned almost anywhere to instantly create a blind – not unlike the stalking-horse used by medieval hunters.

The Use of Smokescreens

The Soviet army made extensive use of smoke during World War II, and continued to do so afterwards. Like most armies, the Soviets used smokescreens to cover an advance or retreat or to protect a bridge or other installation from air attack. The Soviet use of smoke was, however, on a scale that dwarfed any Allied smokescreen. For instance, during the final advance on Berlin, a screen some 300 kilometres (185 miles) long was laid and maintained for five days. The actual area of the crossing was 'only' some 90 kilometres (55 miles) wide, but the huge screen concealed the exact location within a much larger area.

In addition to its defensive capabilities, smoke was used by the Soviets to make the enemy give away his position. The practice of delivering smoke shells onto an enemy position by artillery or mortar in order to cover an assault was commonplace, and many units responded by opening fire into the smoke. This could be effective if the enemy were charging

towards their positions, but the Soviet army used this gambit to locate enemy heavy weapons positions. After the smokescreen was delivered, infantry remained under cover but began shouting and cheering as if they were making an assault. The usual response was a hail of fire from enemy machine guns, which gave away their positions. These were then plastered with return fire before the real assault began.

The ability to generate smoke continued to be of paramount importance to Soviet military planners. Smoke grenade launchers on vehicles – similar to those used by most nations – were supplemented by devices to allow any tank to generate large clouds of smoke by introducing chemicals into the engine

Below: US forces make use of the prevailing wind to deploy a large smoke screen covering the Rhine crossings. Smoke not only conceals what is there, but also what is not. Enemy personnel cannot tell whether they are about to be imminently attacked or if the smoke is a deceptive measure and the attack is to be made elsewhere.

exhaust. During the Cold War years, this was a potential countermeasure to defeat NATO guided antitank missiles. Many such weapons are optically guided and cannot hit what the operator cannot see.

Huge clouds of smoke also force attack helicopters to fly higher, which can make them more vulnerable to air defences. Since one of the main responses to a massed armoured thrust across Europe by the Warsaw Pact was a series of mobile ambushes by tank-killing helicopters, the capability to shroud an advance in smoke translated directly to greater offensive capability.

The Soviet Doctrine of *Maskirovka*

The Russian word *Maskirovka* is sometimes mistranslated as 'camouflage', but in fact covers a range of activities that include camouflage and the related use of dummies and decoys as well as other deceptive measures. *Maskirovka* is a mindset as much as it is a doctrine; it concerns taking every opportunity to confuse and deceive the enemy at every level. Some aspects of *Maskirovka* are unconnected with the science of camouflage, except inasmuch as they make use of camouflage techniques or complement them in working towards the end goal.

Maskirovka aims to ensure that the enemy never has clear and useful data on dispositions, intentions or capabilities, and that he cannot be sure what information he has is trustworthy. Camouflage techniques fit into this doctrine at every level and are routinely practised even when there might seem to be no need. Just as at the outset of World War II, when Soviet infantrymen were indoctrinated with the need to use camouflage and to remain concealed wherever possible, the Red Army of the Cold War era was trained to make use of every possible deceptive measure.

The principles of *Maskirovka* are also the principles of effective camouflage:
• To be effective, a given measure must be active – that is, it must be implemented intelligently and with a useful purpose in mind, and it must be aimed at a particular target.
• *Maskirovka* measures must also be persuasive (or plausible) and must be timely.
• Camouflage must be in place before the enemy obtains his first view of the scene, and must be relevant to the current situation.
• Camouflage measures that are intermittently applied or that are not used properly are likely to be useless.
• Camouflage must also be applied with forethought and creativity.

Using the same methods in the same old way is often ineffective. The enemy will learn what to look for or develop counters to methods that have been seen before. There are limits, of course, to how much variety is possible, and a decision to do exactly the same as last time may be correct. However, repeating previous measures simply out of habit is not acceptable; all camouflage and *Maskirovka* measures must be implemented with the needs of the current situation in mind.

Cold War Developments

Relations between the Western allies and the Soviet Union were never warm, and there were those who advocated pushing on eastwards

Above: Soldiers of the Red Army constructing a field fortification. Digging in is practised by almost every armed force in the world, but few come close to the Russian mindset of concealing every position as much as possible.

after the fall of Germany to eliminate the Soviet Union as a threat before it became too powerful. Conversely, there were those on the other side of the 'Iron Curtain' that slammed down across Europe who considered that a continued offensive westwards was the best option.

The East/West clash never happened, but the possibility of such a conflict was a major driving factor in strategy and equipment design during the Cold War period. Both sides were heavily influenced by their experiences during World

Chronology of Tank Camouflage

The science of concealing tanks has evolved along with the technology for building them. There are, however, limits to what can be achieved with paint, and other methods such as thermal emission modification are now being investigated.

Sturmpanzerwagen A7V (1917)

There was little point in trying to conceal the German A7V tank. Indeed, its best option was to be very obvious and hope to scare the enemy into retreating.

Panzer IV Ausf F (1940)

This Panzer IV Ausf F from early World War II is obvious up close but would fade well into a distant horizon, perhaps allowing it to get close enough to use its short-ranged but powerful gun.

M5 Stuart light tank (1943)

Like most early-war US tanks this M5 Stuart wears a simple olive-drab colour scheme.

T-34 Model 1943 (1944)

This mid-war T-34 has received winter camouflage in the form of a thin whitewash over its green base colour.

Panzer VI Tiger I (1944)

Late-war German tanks like this Tiger I typically left the factory with a *dunkelgelb* colour scheme, to which locally appropriate colours were added.

M48 Patton (1970)

The M48 Patton was deployed by many armies over the course of the 1960s, 70s and 80s. This example, supplied to the Spanish army, wears a two-tone European camouflage scheme.

FV107 Scimitar (1985)

The Scimitar armoured reconnaissance vehicle's best defence is speed and concealment. Its armour is not capable of defeating most anti-tank weapons.

Challenger 2 (2003)

The British Challenger wore a 'light stone' colour scheme whilst deployed in the Middle East – a system that dates back to World War II but which has recently been replaced with a darker brown colour.

T-90 (2004)

The Russian T-90 typically wears a dark green colour scheme, modified when deployed to suit the current operating environment.

War II and for the most part continued the logical development of technology and doctrine with a new opponent in mind.

STRATEGIES OF THE SOVIET UNION

The Soviet Union and its allies sought to maximize their advantages in terms of manpower and industrial production by creating large armoured and other forces of no great technological sophistication. The 'Red Steamroller' had crushed Axis opposition; there was every chance it could do the same to the newly emerging NATO alliance. The Western powers could not match Soviet numbers, so instead sought to compete on a technological basis, meeting quantity with quality.

Experience in World War II indicated that in any future European war it was the tank – or rather, massed tank forces – that would be the decisive weapon. Deep-penetration armoured breakthroughs and exploitation were standard strategies, along with armoured counterattacks to contain them. The Warsaw Pact hoped to achieve victory by rapid offensive action, while the West

had a more defensive strategy in mind – at least for the opening months of a conflict. Once the initial Soviet onslaught had been blunted, counteroffensive operations would become possible.

These differing mindsets are obvious from the equipment and training of forces deployed to Europe during the Cold War. Soviet tanks had a lower silhouette that made them harder targets when on the move. Western tank design emphasized a fairly defensive role, with high turrets that allowed the vehicle to remain hull-down behind concealment or hard cover and to engage the advancing enemy on favourable terms. This was essential to halting the initial assaults, since NATO forces would be heavily outnumbered and facing large forces concentrated against their defensive positions.

STRATEGIES OF NATO AND THE WEST

Western strategies for slowing and ultimately halting the Soviet advance included plans for the defence of urban areas including West Berlin. There was no real chance of preventing the fall of the city, but a resistance had to be prepared. Other cities within West Germany were close enough to Warsaw Pact territory that they would

Left: This M551 Sheridan tank has been prepared to blend into an ambush position. In 1982, when this picture was taken, the primary threat to Europe was a massed Warsaw Pact invasion led by armoured forces. The NATO counter-strategy was to blunt the assault with defensive fighting before counterattacking.

Right: If the time is available, a tank can be camouflaged to the point where it is virtually impossible to see at a distance. The long barrel of the main gun is hard to conceal, but if its outline can be broken up and lost against the backdrop there is a good chance of remaining unobserved.

be attacked long before any reinforcements could arrive, but these cities could serve as bastions to slow or channel any Westward offensive.

The many small towns and villages of the Northern European Plain were also potential points of resistance. It was impossible to defend them all, but an advancing enemy would run the risk of ambush or unexpectedly heavy resistance if it ignored the possibility that any given urban area – however small – was not defended. This strategy could not halt the Warsaw Pact advance but, by wringing as much effect as possible out of every small action, it could be slowed until a coherent response materialized. A key part of that was the arrival of reinforcements across the Atlantic.

NATO's delaying and ultimately defensive strategy made extensive use of concealed and camouflaged positions, much like Axis forces in late World War II. Concealment not only allowed an ambush to be more effective but also helped the defending forces break contact if their positions were threatened. A headlong pursuit of enemies who appeared to be pulling out of their positions might lead into another ambush, forcing commanders to advance far more cautiously or take heavy casualties. Both

aided the Western cause, albeit in different ways. Decoys played an important part in this strategy. Even a simple two-dimensional representation of a tank could confuse reconnaissance troops and create doubt about whether a different tank-like shape glimpsed through trees or down a street was the real thing. More advanced decoys included sound and heat generators to create a more convincing impression.

At best, the use of decoys might cause the enemy to pause and set up a concentrated attack against targets that were not there. This wasted ordnance, delayed the advance, and might also cause the front units to halt where they could be more effectively attacked by air assets or artillery. More commonly, a decoy might distract the enemy from a real tank or installation for a moment, but even such a minor contribution could be significant.

Conversely, a camouflaged vehicle or installation might not be spotted until the enemy was deep in the kill zone. While most armoured vehicles and other units needed camouflage that matched Northern European vegetation, for operations in urban terrain a new kind of

Left: This M60 Patton main battle tank is wearing a blocky Dual-Tex camouflage scheme which is in many ways the forerunner of modern pixellated schemes. Against the backdrop of an urban area the blocks break up the outline whilst also depriving the eye of reference points.

squares around 45 centimetres (18in) in size, in contrasting colours. The squares were found to have an optimum size regardless of the vehicle dimensions they were painted on. Antenna, which were often obvious, could be concealed by breaking them into different-coloured sections.

Against the backdrop of angular urban shapes, Berlin Camouflage was of little use within 50 metres (165ft), but proved highly effective beyond this distance. Vehicles were difficult to make out beyond 100 metres (330ft), and in many cases it was nearly impossible to tell whether the vehicle spotted was a tank, a truck or a land rover, at least for the critical few seconds that might be all an engagement took. British tanks in Berlin were all painted in the same pattern, adding an additional layer of deception by making it difficult for observers to tell how many there were. It is notable that Warsaw Pact vehicles began to appear in a very similar camouflage scheme soon after Berlin Camouflage made its appearance.

Meanwhile, the US Army was using a similar concept named Dual-Texture, or Dual-Tex. This took the standard US camouflage pattern

camouflage was necessary. It was, of course, possible to conceal vehicles in buildings or to use the surroundings to create a 'hide' with some additional camouflage netting. However, this did not solve the problem of camouflage for vehicles that had to move around.

LESSONS FROM BERLIN

Royal Dragoon Guards serving as part of the Berlin Brigade defending West Berlin developed 'Berlin Camouflage' in the early 1980s. The standard dark green used for most British armoured vehicles was replaced by a system of of the time and broke it up into 10 centimetre (4in) squares, creating a micropattern within the main camouflage pattern. Dual-Tex could be applied with a standard paint roller or brush, or stencilled on to a vehicle using something as simple as a brush and a piece of cardboard.

Tests indicated that Dual-Tex camouflage imposed a greater delay on recognition of objects than standard camouflage. It was adopted by the US 2nd Armored Cavalry Regiment in 1979 and was used until the adoption of the new three-colour standard in the late 1980s. The concept of a micropattern within a macropattern was later reused by Lieutenant-Colonel Timothy O'Neil, the inventor of Dual-Tex, to create digital infantry camouflage. Various myths sprang up about Dual-Tex, notably that it was designed to exploit the characteristics of Soviet optics. Although these claims were untrue, Dual-Tex did provide effective camouflage for its environment.

Below: British Chieftain tanks parade through West Berlin, 1989. The tanks are painted in 'Berlin Camouflage' – large squares of contrasting colour.

Concealing Fortifications and other Installations

Methods also had to be found to conceal bunkers and other installations within urban areas. A reinforced building can be rather obvious if left as bare concrete with weapon emplacements here and there, and a forest of antenna might also be difficult to conceal. One option was to use external camouflage in the form of cladding designed to look like brickwork. Camouflage was of limited use if the enemy knew where the installation was located, but even so it might confuse an attacker long enough for the bunker's weapons to open fire.

The art of concealing bunkers and other fortifications had been developed by most nations in World War II. The British underwent a period of defensive preparation in 1939–40, when invasion seemed likely, and constructed a large number of defensive structures. Not all were camouflaged; to this day, simple concrete pillboxes can be spotted all across the country covering roads and river crossings. Although not camouflaged, many of these installations are protected or partially concealed by terrain

Left: These bunkers in Switzerland, like many others, are designed to resemble a natural rocky feature. Switzerland's extensive fortifications were carefully blended into the countryside, taking advantage of terrain for concealment as well as to offer good fields of fire.

from many angles. Similarly, the Japanese fortified many Pacific islands, often using natural materials to build bunkers that were by their very nature difficult to spot.

Switzerland, though not a belligerent in either World War and neutral in the Cold War, was extensively fortified. Bunkers and weapon emplacements were ingeniously disguised as houses, barns or rocky outcrops. Many of these installations made use of naturally occurring positions overlooking roads, railways and river crossings, and blended perfectly into the landscape. Combined with the Alpine terrain and a heavily armed population, Switzerland's bunker systems provided an excellent deterrent to aggression.

Fortifications have traditionally served to defend against ground attack, or to cover strategic sections of coastline. However, during the Cold War era it was obvious that any conflict would take the form of an 'air/land battle' in which air power and mobile ground forces would complement one another. Air defence installations, such as radar sites and missile batteries, formed an integral part of the ground defences of Europe, providing an umbrella under which friendly ground forces could operate with reduced chance of air attack. Conversely, any installation designed for participation in the ground war was likely to face air attack.

Installations located far to the rear were likely targets for long-range strike and bomber aircraft, while those closer to the front were more likely to be attacked by the same low-flying strike aircraft that carried out battlefield support operations or perhaps attack helicopters. A measure of defence was possible using missiles and guns, and of course air superiority forces might stop some of the strikes. However, it was inevitable that military installations would be attacked from the air as part of a ground campaign. One of the measures adopted to protect installations in Western Europe was 'toning down', whereby the contrast between the installation and its surroundings was reduced. Buildings were camouflaged or painted in disruptive shapes that made them more difficult to discern, while roads, runways and other distinctive features were also 'toned down' to make them less obvious. Vegetation planted around an installation not only made it look more natural but blocked some angles of

observation; at the same time, the roofs of some buildings were given a false urban profile to simulate a small village or other innocuous site.

Toning down was not intended to completely conceal the existence of an installation; it was too much to hope that any but the most secret installations might escape observation in the long term. Its purpose was to make the installation difficult to positively identify, and

Below: An M551 Sheridan tank in MERDC camouflage. The Mobility Equipment Research & Design Command (MERDC) produced a series of standardised camouflage schemes for US vehicles in the 1970s. The underlying concept was to enable a vehicle to be quickly repainted to suit a new deployment, by altering only those areas necessary. MERDC camouflage used a system of twelve colours to create sufficient combinations for many different environments.

thereby to reduce the chances of an attack from the air. In the event of such an attack, the difficulty of determining the most effective point at which to aim weapons might permit the installation to survive.

Modern Vehicle Camouflage

The US military became interested in camouflage for its vehicles during the 1960s, but it was not until 1974–75 that camouflage was officially adopted. Up until that point, olive drab was the standard colour for military vehicles, although the exact specification for olive drab varied over time. Some vehicles were camouflaged before 1975, although usually on a local and ad-hoc basis.

The four-colour patterns adopted in 1975 are sometimes referred to as MERDC, for the Mobility Equipment Research and Development Centre operated by the army. These were standard on US army vehicles until the mid-1980s, when NATO countries standardized a three-colour camouflage system. The adoption of a single system was for a very good reason – to deny information to the enemy. Up until that point, it was possible to determine which NATO countries were operating in an area by their camouflage patterns, even if they were using the same vehicles and taking pains to conceal their nationality. A common camouflage system deprived the opposition of this capability.

NATO camouflage of this era was sometimes referred to as CARC (Chemical Agent Resistant Coating), and made use of three colours. Black and green were combined with red-brown to create standardized patterns, which could be adapted for winter use by overpainting part or all of the black areas in white. The greens used by various nations varied; Germany favoured *bronzgrun* (bronze-green), while the US military preferred a darker shade.

For desert operations, a single-shade tan colouring was standardized within NATO. Vehicles intended for units operating in temperate areas left the factory painted solid-green, but since 1991 the vast majority of operations have been in desert areas, resulting in vehicles supplied painted tan instead. However, at the time of writing, emphasis is shifting back to operations in Europe, with temperate camouflage becoming the default.

Below: A French Leclerc main battle tank, wearing a three-tone colour scheme well suited to conditions in Northern Europe. The practice of camouflaging combat vehicles has been in place in France since well before World War II.

Above: These Chinese ZTD-05 amphibious tanks feature a pixellated 'maritime' colour scheme. It has also been suggested that the colours could be rapidly replaced in the same pattern by a computer-controlled process, tailoring the camouflage scheme to various environments.

This does not mean that operations in desert areas will cease in the immediate future. Indeed, another recent development in the British army is the implementation of a new colour scheme for this region. After decades of using a 'light stone' or 'dark yellow' colouring for vehicles intended for desert operations, the British army has moved to a shade called 'army brown'. The paint used for this new colour scheme is designed to react to certain compounds, acting as a warning against chemical weapons contamination.

Russian armoured vehicles are typically given camouflage suited to their expected operating environment, usually with greens and browns on a tan base colour, although this can vary. These schemes are conventional in nature and are probably based on long experience in the field. On the other hand, the Chinese military has recently begun using pixellated designs, some in bold colours such as blues and greys.

It is possible that these patterns are intended to provide concealment in snowy environments or when conducting amphibious operations. However, many observers have suggested that this colouration is not camouflage at all but ostentation. Tanks and other vehicles wearing these patterns have appeared in military parades, which fits with this theory. It seems likely that a different version of these pixellated patterns, perhaps in a less obvious colour scheme, might be used for combat operations. Such colour schemes do exist and have been observed on Chinese armoured vehicles.

Advances in Vehicle Camouflage

In the modern environment, optical detection is not the only threat faced by armoured vehicles; indeed, it may not be the main threat. Thermal imaging is available at all levels, down to individual soldiers, and the thermal emissions of an armoured vehicle are far more obvious than its visual signature. Camouflage paintwork is of little use if the vehicle is visible by other means.

Concealing this thermal signature is difficult. It is possible to screen emissions from hot exhausts and components such as the engine from some angles, but the vehicle itself is likely to be much warmer than its surroundings and thus rather obvious. Until recently, the only viable option was to position the vehicle behind a completely opaque barrier. Camouflage netting would not suffice; only a solid object would hide a tank's thermal signature.

However, recently emerging technologies have created alternatives. An experimental system exists that can conceal or even disguise the vehicle's thermal characteristics. The outer surface of the vehicle is covered in panels that can be controlled to emit whatever level of heat is required. This can be matched to the local ambient conditions – which are constantly monitored by thermal cameras on the vehicle – or can be set to mimic a specific object.

This capability enables an armoured vehicle to engage in either crypsis or mimicry, and can allow a tank to seem to be an ordinary car or some other object to thermal sensors. The ability to mimic other vehicles is important – a thermally 'blank' area might escape notice if static, whereas one that is unaccountably moving will attract attention. On the other hand, a thermal signature that is detected and identified as an ordinary car may well be ignored. This follows one of the basic tenets of camouflage operations: the disguise must be plausible.

This system has applications beyond disguising the thermal signature of armoured vehicles. Permanent structures could be concealed in the same manner, or the same

Below: Optical camouflage does nothing to hide an armoured vehicle from thermal imaging. Engines, guns and tracks all generate heat, which can reveal a vehicle that is all but invisible to the naked eye. During the Gulf War, this method was used to find targets by Coalition aircraft engaging in tank destroying at night.

system might be modified for use by a warship. It is possible that if the technology can be adapted to work in more wavelengths than just thermal radiation it might become an 'invisibility cloak' for vehicles rather than only masking their thermal signature. However, that alone is a useful goal. Thermal detection is the greatest threat on the battlefield, and up to now no counter for vehicles on the move has been available.

Acoustic (noise) signature is less of a problem for vehicles than thermal detection, but there are still situations in which a tank or other vehicle can give away its presence by the sound of its engine and tracks. The recent invention of various 'acoustic metamaterials' makes it possible to control the propagation of sound to a greater extent than ever before. Applications for the military include concealing the sound of generators and vehicle engines, and perhaps even gunfire.

This would have important implications for urban warfare in particular, where

Above: The Polish PL-01 is sometimes described as a 'stealth tank' whose features include a greatly reduced radar return as well as the ability to manipulate its thermal emissions. This is an emerging technology which will likely see increased use in the future, giving armoured vehicles much greater protection from targetting systems.

engagement ranges tend to be short. The sound of an approaching armoured vehicle, or one starting up ready to attack, can be sufficient for enemy personnel to take cover or to set up an ambush. Power generation for communications and air defence equipment can also be located acoustically.

Enemy positions can sometimes be pinpointed by the sound of activity there or shots fired from them. This is difficult in an urban environment where sound echoes from multiple hard surfaces, but with new acoustic technology it might become all but impossible. One potential application is to permit snipers to operate without anyone but the target (and those close by) being aware of the shots.

CHAPTER 4

CAMOUFLAGE IN AIR WARFARE

The development of camouflage to protect aircraft and ground targets has proceeded at an astonishing pace to reach its present level of sophistication.

At the outbreak of the Great War, air power was very much in its infancy. The ability of aircraft to attack ground targets had already been established, but the new arm had yet to truly find its niche. It was not yet proven, for example, that an aircraft could sink a warship either in port or underway in the open sea.

What was obvious was that aircraft could conduct reconnaissance operations quite deep into enemy territory, returning with information more quickly than a ground patrol. Even given the frequent breakdowns of aircraft in the era, air reconnaissance was still as reliable as using cavalry, which could be intercepted and prevented from reaching its objective or returning with a timely report.

Opposite: The B2 Spirit Bomber personifies an era in which visual detection is no longer the main threat to an aircraft. Its black colouration offers some concealment against a dark sky, but its primary defences are against thermal and radar systems.

The large ammunition and supply dumps behind the trench lines, as well as artillery positions and the movements of reserve forces, were difficult to observe at ground level but very obvious from the air. This had several implications. The buildup to an offensive was hard to conceal, but air reconnaissance could provide an indication of precisely what forces the enemy had deployed and therefore some idea of his intentions. Artillery positions and logistics dumps, once found, could be shelled by long-range artillery whose performance could be readily assessed by a reconnaissance aircraft.

Observation balloons could provide some of these capabilities, but aircraft covered a wider area and extended range of vision much deeper into enemy territory. Countering this capability on the part of the enemy quickly became a priority. Indeed, many of the early camoufleurs started their careers by camouflaging artillery positions against airborne observation.

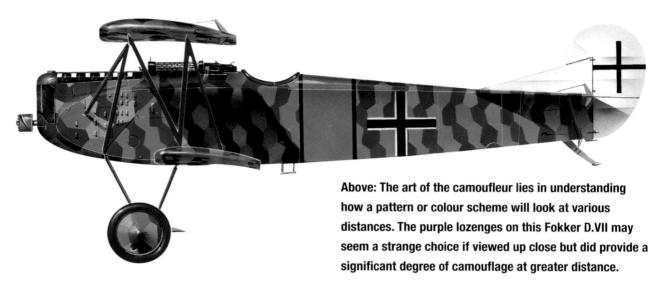

Above: The art of the camoufleur lies in understanding how a pattern or colour scheme will look at various distances. The purple lozenges on this Fokker D.VII may seem a strange choice if viewed up close but did provide a significant degree of camouflage at greater distance.

Although passive measures such as camouflage screens were at best a partial success, both sides quickly learned to make the best of them and to use camouflage netting to enhance the natural concealment of their chosen positions. Ammunition dumps and artillery positions were increasingly set up in wooded areas, which provided a measure of natural concealment. However, a more active defence was desirable. Anti-aircraft weapons were improvised from multiple machine-gun mounts and light, quick-firing guns, and soon began to be custom built. In time, these would come under attack and be protected by their own camouflage.

Camouflaging Reconnaissance Aircraft

A more proactive approach to denying the enemy air reconnaissance data was provided by aircraft themselves. Pilots began attacking one another with their service revolvers (sometimes literally; there are accounts of aircrew attempting to throw their empty guns into the propellers of enemy aircraft), along with an array of shotguns, rifles and even the occasional brick.

These amateurish measures quickly gave way to purpose-built combat aircraft armed with one or more machine guns. Originally termed 'scouts', single-seat aircraft became 'fighters' whose purpose was to shoot down their opposite numbers, to intercept bombers and reconnaissance aircraft, and sometimes to carry out ground attacks of their own.

Camouflage measures were applied to these early combat aircraft, mainly to make them more difficult to spot (and perhaps attack) from the air while they were on the ground. Many aircraft used by the Central Powers had their upper surfaces camouflaged with an irregular pattern of lozenges or other geometric shapes to break up the distinctive straight lines of the wings and fuselage. The influence of the Cubist movement in this development was considerable.

Lozenge camouflage often used fairly bright colours on the underside of aircraft, with darker shades on surfaces likely to be seen from above. Lozenge camouflage was sometimes painted on aircraft but was also applied in the form of cloth, which was then used to cover the aircraft.

French and German aircraft were given a brown and green camouflage pattern, but this caused identification problems. The solution applied by German air units was to substitute patches of purple for brown. Despite sounding counterintuitive, this worked well at longer ranges while up close it assisted in identifying an aircraft as friendly. The British also experimented with brown and green for the upper surfaces of aircraft, and attempted to create night camouflage using black undersides. When this proved to be too dark, a variety of shades were tried. A grey-green colour named NIVO (Night Invisible Varnish Oxfordness, for the Oxfordness research station where it was developed) was applied, and remained in use into the 1930s.

Strategies for Aircraft Camouflage

Aircraft operate in an environment of considerable contrasts. Seen from above, or from the side when on the ground, an aircraft typically stood against a background of natural colours that were predominantly green and brown. From below, the backdrop varied from blue sky and white to grey clouds to the near black of night.

This created a problem when creating aircraft camouflage, not least because the rapid movement of an aircraft might take it over several different types of terrain during a mission, while weather conditions could quickly change from bright sunlight and blue skies to dark grey cloud or poor visibility due to rain. Attempts to create invisible, transparent aircraft were – perhaps predictably – unsuccessful.

Wings and similar components could be made out of transparent materials, but this did not greatly reduce the aircraft's visual signature; in fact, it might at times increase it due to reflected sunlight.

Metal components and windscreens (or later, canopies) in an aircraft would reflect light and perhaps draw attention to the aircraft, and a low-flying aircraft could also be betrayed by its shadow. Little could be done about that, but the aircraft itself could be camouflaged. One option was to paint the upper surfaces of an aircraft in colours that matched the terrain and the underside to be less visible against the sky. That, however, was not an easy undertaking. Simple blue or white stood out too much, resulting in experimentation with various shades of grey. Similarly, a black-painted aircraft was found to

Below: The idea of using black as a camouflage colour against the night sky seems obvious, but it turned out to be ineffective – a plane that was blacker than the background stood out to an unacceptable degree. NIVO camouflage more closely approximated the background and thus concealed the aircraft much better.

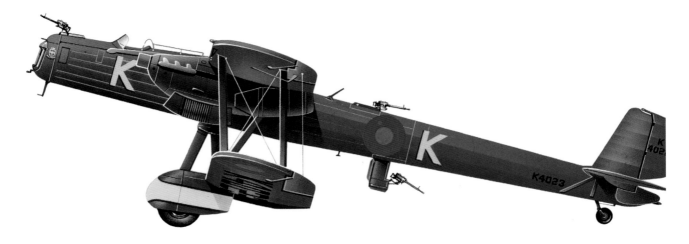

Flying Aces in Colourful Aircraft

Not everyone believed in the benefits of concealment. This was the era of the 'Red Baron', Manfred von Richthofen, and similar pioneers of air combat. Richthofen believed that it was the pilot that mattered, not the quality of his aircraft, and encouraged his peers to paint their aircraft in distinctive colours. This boosted morale on both sides, with the appearance of certain aircraft striking fear into their opponents and encouraging their allies. Flying a brightly coloured or distinctively patterned aircraft made the pilot a target in more than one sense. Famous pilots became priority targets for up-and-coming 'aces' seeking to establish a reputation, and their aircraft were easy to spot. It is perhaps telling that the era of brightly coloured fighters was short, and was replaced with dowdy camouflage paint.

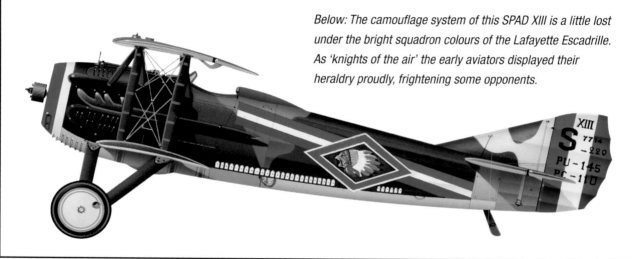

Below: The camouflage system of this SPAD XIII is a little lost under the bright squadron colours of the Lafayette Escadrille. As 'knights of the air' the early aviators displayed their heraldry proudly, frightening some opponents.

be very visible at night, as it stood out as darker than the surrounding sky.

Some military aircraft are designed to operate close to the ground, and thus require the same sort of camouflage as ground vehicles. This must be tailored to local conditions; a scheme of greens and browns is useful in temperate regions or where there is a lot of vegetation. Sandy colours are more useful over desert. Naval strike aircraft may operate over land or water. If the latter, greys and blues are effective, whereas aircraft intended to attack targets inland might be better camouflaged for conditions there.

Camouflage can help ground-attack aircraft

to evade detection from above and below, providing the aircraft remains sufficiently low to avoid being silhouetted against the sky. A fast-moving object such as an aircraft is hard to conceal at close range – and draws a lot of attention due to its engine noise – but from greater distances, ground-colour camouflage can offer real benefits.

For higher-flying aircraft, ground-colour camouflage was less useful, although it was still often considered beneficial to use darker colours on the upper surfaces of an aircraft, which might be less visible against the ground or sea, and lighter colours underneath. Although not of much use at close range, a well-chosen colour scheme helped the aircraft to fade into the hazy distance. A pinkish-grey was considered by many wartime camouflage experts to offer the best concealment.

Although some camouflaged objects – and people, such as snipers and observers – might hope to evade detection entirely, this is not possible for aircraft. Even modern 'stealth' designs are not invisible. What camouflage and

other colours do is to reduce the distance at which the aircraft is likely to be first detected, and to make it harder to track for enemy pilots or gunners.

Camouflage has been deemed less important than identification in some situations, such as German aircraft during the Battle of Britain and Allied aircraft during the invasion of Normandy. With large forces committed against an enemy that was on full alert, camouflage offered limited advantages compared to a reduction in 'friendly fire' incidents. Thus, many aircraft were painted in ways that made them relatively easy to spot, such as the bright yellow nose of many German fighters or the 'invasion stripes' on the wings of Allied aircraft. Aircraft operating away from the main combat areas might benefit from

Below: This Spitfire is wearing 'invasion stripes' whilst operating over the Normandy beachheads in 1944. With such intense military activity going on, identification was deemed more important than concealment – a throwback perhaps to the days of red jackets and brightly coloured cockades.

being more stealthy, but those hurled into the maelstrom of fighters and defensive ground fire were better protected by having only one side's guns aimed at them.

In an effort to protect aircrews and onboard systems from the effects of nuclear weapons they had just delivered, some aircraft flew with a bare-metal or polished sliver finish. The increased visibility of the aircraft was considered a necessary tradeoff; the reflective metal was expected to reduce the thermal and radiation effects of nuclear detonation.

Countershading was an effective measure in camouflaging aircraft, generally using lighter tones on lower surfaces and darker ones on those receiving more illumination. However, the reduction of shadow created by countershading was of limited use on an aircraft that undertook a lot of manoeuvres and thereby caused moving shadows on its surfaces.

For aircraft travelling in a straight line much of the time, countershading was more effective, but did not make the aircraft invisible. In an attempt to improve on this kind of camouflage, the US Air Force undertook a series of experiments with 'Yehudi lights', a concept influenced by Canadian Navy experiments in counterillumination.

Yehudi lights were used to lighten the aircraft to match the ambient light level, thus doing away with the common problem of an aircraft being darker than the dark sky beyond. Yehudi lights had to be combined with a suitable colour scheme, and had to be carefully matched to the background. This proved technically difficult, and although the experiments were promising the concept was not practical on a large scale. Nevertheless, the idea of counterillumination was revived in the Vietnam War era, and again in more recent times.

Left: 'Yehudi lights' mounted on an aircraft's outer extremities, matched the illumination of the aircraft to the ambient light conditions, rendering it very difficult to see. The concept was promising but was overtaken by postwar developments in radar and infrared detection.

An Alternative to Camouflage: Bare Metal

There are alternatives to camouflage that offer other benefits. Some reconnaissance aircraft and bombers during World War II were stripped down to the bare metal. Paint does not weigh much, but a tiny reduction in weight equated to a small increase in speed. With armament and armour removed, reconnaissance aircraft could often carry out their mission and escape before a response materialized, or could flee from aircraft of an equivalent class that were burdened more heavily.

Above: Once the Allies had won air superiority over Europe, camouflage became less important. These B-17s benefit from a small reduction in weight and drag due to not carrying paint.

Camouflage on the Ground

The easiest way to eliminate aircraft is to attack them on the ground. As early as the Great War, strikes by bombers and fighter-bombers were launched against enemy air bases. During World War II, such attacks were commonplace and could be devastating. Indeed, had the Luftwaffe concentrated on British fighter bases rather than shifting its strikes to the cities, the Battle of Britain might well have had a different outcome.

Defences against enemy air attack included dispersing aircraft to minimize the effects of a strike and building revetments that would protect against the blast and fragmentation effects of a near miss. Little could be done against a direct hit, but few bombs of the era were so well targeted.

Further protection could be granted by camouflaging the revetments and the aircraft themselves. Attacks were typically made either from quite a high altitude or by aircraft that were flying low and fast under heavy fire. In the first case, distance made it difficult to pick out targets and in the second there was limited time to acquire a suitable target and set up an attack run. It might be that a pilot simply could not get onto a suitable vector in time to make his attack and would then have the choice between aborting

the attack or going around again – increasing the time his own aircraft spent under fire.

A camouflaged installation made the attackers' task more difficult, but the very best defence is not to be attacked at all. If the enemy could not find the target – or they had no idea it was there at all – then an attack could not take place. It was rarely possible to completely conceal an installation, but a combination of camouflage and deception might be sufficient to protect it. Camouflage of ground installations and aircraft followed the same principles as concealing any other installation or vehicle. The distinctive shapes of aircraft had to be disguised, but also the details of the installation, which could help the enemy target its air assets or their supporting fuel and ammunition storage areas.

Attempts to Conceal Runways

Runways were particularly difficult to conceal. A long, straight section of what appeared to be a road that went nowhere could be little else than a runway. One option was to colour the runway to blend in with local conditions, but this was difficult to do convincingly. Alternatively, an airbase could be protected by making it seem like an inoffensive collection of structures such as a farm or small town.

Such a deception could be at least partly accomplished by painting the structures in such a way that their real nature was concealed. A 'false roof' could be created with nothing more than colouring and shading, giving the impression of a three-dimensional structure of a completely different shape or even 'creating' one where none existed.

Light materials were used to construct false walls and other structures, along with fake field boundaries, fences and other peripheral supports to the main camouflage effort. Depending on what level of deception was intended, such a camouflage effort could be quite rudimentary or very elaborate. If the intent was to make it hard for enemy strike aircraft to find an airbase they knew was present, quite basic measures might be sufficient. The effort required to conceal a base or other installation in the long term was far more complex.

Not all of these camouflage operations were successful. Fake airfields were built by both sides during World War II in the hope of deflecting at least part of the enemy effort away from the real ones. Some of these may have been quite successful, especially if they were located close to a real target and would thus confuse attacking aircrew as they approached the target area. However, it was hard to conceal the construction of a new installation from enemy reconnaissance aircraft, and in at least some cases the photographs they took revealed what was really going on. There is a tale, probably apocryphal, of a complete fake airbase created by the Luftwaffe in northern France. Built from wood, it had a control tower, hangars, runways and supporting buildings. The Allies waited until

it was finished, then 'attacked' it with a single wooden bomb.

Whether or not this tale is true, it serves to illustrate the difficulty of creating something false where the enemy could see it being built. The fake airbase might still have served a useful purpose if it attracted the odd raid – bombers in that era found it very difficult to navigate to the target and not infrequently became lost. Rather than take their bombs home, a crew would seek an alternative target and an airbase would seem inviting. The creation of fake targets was an important countermeasure to the immense bombing campaigns of World War II.

Countering the Bombers

A bombing raid in World War II required a long flight to the target, during which the bombers might become lost or confused about their position. The RAF decided early in the war that daylight strategic bombing raids

Below: It is difficult to camouflage an aircraft hangar to look like anything else, mainly due to its sheer size. However, hangars can be made to look like a row of houses or other structures that would not be singled out for a bombing attack.

were extremely dangerous, and shifted to night operations. This increased the difficulty in navigating to the target area even as it improved bomber survivability.

Many raids were led to their target by the lead bombers, whose navigators calculated a course by dead reckoning and took account of wind conditions as best they could. Since the course usually involved crossing the sea, a large part of the flight was made without much in the way of navigational reference points. Therefore, when the enemy coast was sighted its landmarks were used to calculate a position and if necessary plan a new route to the target. Rivers, coastal towns and similar features were used to obtain a position, but these could easily be misidentified.

There were even cases of bombers detached from the rest of the raid and proceeding alone becoming so lost that they returned over their friendly coast thinking they had entered enemy territory. Some of these bombers found a promising target and made an attack before realizing their error.

Most crews did not become this badly lost, but simply finding the target area was a major challenge. This was compounded by a policy of camouflaging or even removing landmarks. Distinctive features were hidden as well as possible, sometimes making it impossible to tell whether the bombers were over the right city.

Bodies of water were a useful landmark, and were often highlighted in briefings delivered to the crews before takeoff. Knowing this, camoufleurs on the ground sought to disguise them by depositing a film of coal dust on the surface or creating a fake body of water a short distance away. This technique was used by both British and German camoufleurs, who in some cases went to great lengths to disguise important landmarks. A lake or other distinctive body of water could be disguised by floating rafts upon it, which were covered in dummy structures that resembled houses or factories.

Major roads and rail links were disguised where possible by covering them over with plywood painted to look like the roofs of houses, and fake bridges were constructed while real ones were camouflaged. During night raids, bombers commonly found their targets by looking for the fires started by the first aircraft in the raid. A counter to this was to light fires a short distance away from the target city in the hope that at least some of the bombers would attack empty fields by mistake.

Disguising Critical Installations

Some staggeringly complex camouflage operations were undertaken during World War II to protect critical installations. The Lockheed factory in Burbank and the Boeing factory at Seattle were considered to be possible targets for Japanese air attack. Although they were never bombed, there was no way of knowing this, so measures were taken to conceal them.

These large installations were disguised by effectively building a fake town over the top. Roads and buildings were created, with high structures used as the basis for a 'hill' on whose flanks the fake town stood. Under the camouflage, car parks for the workers operated as normal and work went on as usual.

German attempts to conceal critical installations suggest that such elaborate concealment measures may or may not have been effective if the factories had been attacked. If the enemy possessed reconnaissance photographs of the area before the camouflage operation was undertaken, it might be possible to calculate a bomb drop point using landmarks that were not concealed, or to saturate the general area and thus obtain a few hits at least.

Above: Bomb aiming was a difficult task, especially at night over a blacked-out target. A common tactic was to send the first wave of bombers in with incendiaries, so that subsequent waves could take aim on the fires. Of course, this required that the first bombs were properly targeted, otherwise the whole raid might miss the target.

Experience on the Axis side suggested that concealing the real installation and creating a plausible fake nearby was sometimes effective.

The fake needed to be close to the real target, however. If the bomb aimer saw what looked like the target a few seconds early, he might be fooled into attacking it instead; if it was too far out of position he would doubt its reality and not waste his bombs.

It has also been suggested that, early in the war, bombing accuracy was so bad that camouflage might actually increase the chances of a hit. The vast majority of bombs fell nowhere

Night Bombing

The difficulties of bombing in World War II are illustrated by the story of a crew who became separated from their squadron and very lost over the North Sea. Sighting the enemy coast ahead, they looked for landmarks and eventually realised they must be nowhere near the target. There was nothing recognisable in the blacked-out countryside, but as they searched they spotted what looked like a fighter airfield.

Not wanting to waste their ordnance but now low on fuel, the crew resolved to make an attack. Targeting was difficult but the bombs were delivered, apparently on target, and the bomber crossed the coast headed out to sea. Alone in the night, they became lost once again. Flying on guesswork, the navigator somehow got them to a familiar section of coast from where they were able to find their way home. Exhausted, the crew went to sleep.

The next morning they were awakened by a demand from the commanding officer of a nearby fighter base to explain why they had bombed his airfield – and one from their own commander who wanted to know why they had not done any damage.

Camouflage of this nature was of some value, but against the massed bomber raids of World War II there was a limit to what could be achieved. The Luftwaffe attempted to use electronic systems to guide its bombers and thereby gave the Allies the means to reliably misdirect them. By using intersecting radio beams, German bombers were informed of exactly the right point to release their weapons. This proved very effective and completely negated any attempt to visually conceal the targets – at least until the Allies were able to electronically conceal them as well by jamming the guidance signals.

Other measures used to protect bomber targets included making them look as if the damage caused by a previous raid had not been repaired. The runways of many airbases were painted with fake craters, while those nearby were not repaired. The hope was that reconnaissance photographs would show the base as non-operational and thereby cause the enemy to target something else. This worked some of the time, although skilled analysts could discern between a three-dimensional crater and a two-dimensional representation of one.

Protecting Airbases after World War II

Experience of attacks upon airbases led to attempts to create greater survivability in future. During the Cold War, it was – correctly – assumed that any attack by either side would begin with an attempt to eliminate air power in the combat region. Airbases were obvious targets for an early strike. Some measures had been tried before, such as the creation of dummy aircraft. Models made of cheap materials or even inflatable dummies were deployed. Although less than convincing to

near the target due to poor aiming equipment, so confusing bomb aimers about where the target actually was might result in a random hit. Later in the war, with more accurate aiming systems, a fake target was more useful, especially since a formation would often aim at the lead bomber's target. A fake might be accurately attacked by an entire formation and thus save the real target.

Above: The Lockheed plant at Burbank, California, and the co-located Burbank Union airport, were protected from the possibility of Japanese bombing by a huge camouflage operation. This entire area of what appears to be innocuous suburb is fake, covering a major aircraft manufacturing facility.

someone standing nearby, these dummies could possibly fool a strike pilot travelling at high speed while under fire. Even a split second of confusion could result in wasted weapons and the survival of real aircraft hidden not far away.

The British went to great lengths to create a combat aircraft that could survive such an attack on NATO airbases. The result was the Hawker Harrier, whose vectored thrust capability enabled it to make a very short takeoff run or even take off and land vertically with a reduced warload. Harriers could operate from improvised facilities in the event that airbases were destroyed, or could be dispersed and hidden – yet still remain operational – if an attack seemed imminent.

Most modern combat aircraft require a long, straight runway that could be easily (if temporarily) put out of commission by a few craters. Harriers, on the other hand, could be concealed in a forest clearing or operated from an improvised base such as a barn. With so many possible hiding places available, the chances of a Harrier force being found and attacked were greatly diminished.

Aircraft Camouflage during World War II

Camouflage was used in widely varying forms during World War II, from night-fighter patterns to maritime blues and winter whitewash.

LUFTWAFFE AIRCRAFT CAMOUFLAGE

The evolution of Luftwaffe aircraft camouflage during World War II offers an insight into different requirements and the measures used to meet them. In the early months of the war, and particularly during the Battle of Britain, German fighters often had bright yellow recognition patterns (typically on the nose and tail), since identification was considered more important than concealment. A two-

Above: This German Messerschmitt Me 262 is camouflaged for use as a night fighter. Its grey and black colour scheme is designed to disappear into a cloudy sky, enabling the pilot to choose his target at leisure from among a bomber stream and attack by surprise.

tone grey pattern became more common from 1941 onwards, sometimes with dappled areas to reduce contrast between different shades. Recognition patches became smaller or were omitted entirely, although national insignia remained in place.

Towards the end of the war, German fighters were in grave danger of being attacked on the ground by the overwhelming air power of the Allies, and moved to a ground camouflage pattern (typically irregular patterns of green and brown) intended to conceal them when observed from above. This was a defensive measure, whereas earlier camouflage was intended to improve effectiveness in air combat and could be considered 'offensive' camouflage.

Below: This Dornier Do 17 displays the prominent yellow identification markings used by the Luftwaffe in the early part of World War II. Like many strike platforms, it has a grey underside to help it hide from fighters waiting at high altitude to 'bounce' the bombers.

Japan's ad hoc Approach

Japanese aircraft were typically not camouflaged at the beginning of the war. Navy fighters wore grey and army aircraft were painted a uniform green for the most part. A variety of camouflage patterns emerged later, although there may not have been a standardized doctrine. Bare metal was common on the underside of aircraft, and by the late war materials such as paint were in short supply so aircraft might not receive any camouflage or other paintwork at all.

Kawasaki Ki-61 Hien 'Tony'

This Ki-61 'Tony' was used for air defence of the Home Islands. Its rather confusing mix of blue panels and speckled green/white camouflage seems unlikely to be effective.

Mitsubishi A6M2 Reisen 'Zeke'

The Mitsubishi A6M 'Zeke' or 'Zero' was an extremely effective carrier-based fighter. It flew in many colour schemes, many of which were largely white.

Mitsubishi J2M Raiden 'Jack'

As a land-based interceptor, the Mitsubishi J2M 'Jack' was camouflaged to protect it from attacks on its airfield, and from observation from above whilst climbing to make an interception.

Mitsubishi G4M1 Model 11

The Mitsubishi G4M was a land-based aircraft used for both ground and maritime strike operations. Since many missions involved flight over water, a hazy grey-green colour offered good concealment.

Above: A Halifax Mk III bomber camouflaged for night operations. Losses early in the war caused RAF Bomber Command to switch to night bombing despite the corresponding loss of accuracy.

Below: A Spitfire Mk IA aerial view. Seen from above against the fields of Southern England, the camouflage scheme conceals the distinctive edges of the aircraft and makes it difficult both to spot it and determine its direction and speed.

BRITISH AIRCRAFT CAMOUFLAGE

British aircraft mostly used standardized camouflage patterns to match their environment. In temperate regions, this meant wavy patterns of brown and green on upper surfaces and light blue undersides. As with other nations, aircraft operating in desert environments used sandy tones. The Fleet Air Arm used greys for upper surfaces and light blue underneath. Over time, British aircraft camouflage evolved to match the needs of the conflict. Later-war fighters often wore grey and green, with a matte 'night black' camouflage for night-time operations. Bombers also wore night black on the undersides, with earth and vegetation tones on the upper surfaces.

British reconnaissance units had more leeway than other squadrons in terms of their camouflage colours. Various schemes were tried, but as a general rule blue or grey was popular for high-altitude operations. For lower-level work, pink was found to be effective camouflage colouration. Indeed, some British strike aircraft were painted pink as recently as the Gulf War. This is most effective in the poor light conditions around dawn and dusk, when many reconnaissance operations are carried out.

French aircraft used a generally similar camouflage pattern to the British, although after the conquest of France air units serving the Vichy government were given very prominent red and yellow stripes for identification that effectively negated any camouflage they had. Italy had no standardized camouflage system until 1941, using a mix of browns, greens and yellows before settling on a brown/green upper surface scheme with grey undersides.

SOVIET AIRCRAFT CAMOUFLAGE

Similarly, Soviet aircraft started the war painted in simple blue and green, and received camouflage later. Most camouflage efforts were applied at the factory using whatever paint was available. Although by late 1943 a standardized camouflage system had been

Below: The Lavochkin LaGG-3 (top) is painted in an unusual black and green scheme, designed to provide camouflage when on the ground. The MiG-3 (bottom) is painted in typical winter colours for the Eastern Front.

formulated, it was not followed by most units or aircraft manufacturers.

Russian aircraft operated in a wide range of environments and wore camouflage to match it. This ranged from white arctic camouflage to temperate browns and greens, with two-tone grey being common for air superiority units. Bombers and ground-attack planes typically had blue undersides, or black for night operations.

US AIRCRAFT CAMOUFLAGE

The United States started the war using plain olive drab with grey undersides, although camouflage similar to British patterns was adopted for desert operations. Naval aircraft used shades of grey and grey-blue. Later in the war, many aircraft were not camouflaged at all. This was deemed unnecessary due to the dominance of Allied air power. Bare metal was not uncommon, although Navy aircraft used an all-over sea blue scheme that persisted into the early Cold War era.

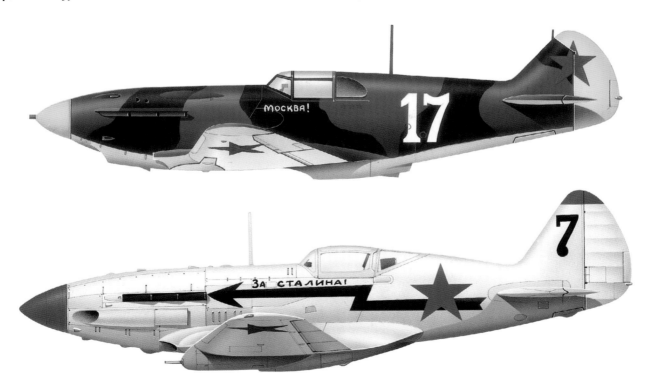

US aviators knew the value of painting the section of fuselage in front of the pilot in a dark matte colour to reduce glare, and were also keen on nose art. Other nations painted designs on their aircraft, or added patriotic slogans here and there, but US aviators took this much further. Nose art varied from shark's teeth to half-dressed women, and was more about pride and morale than concealment.

NIGHT CAMOUFLAGE OF AIRCRAFT

Night camouflage became extremely important for both sides as the war went on. German aircraft typically used different tones of grey, often in irregular patterns, but black was also

Above: The P-51 Mustang became famous for escorting bombers on long-range missions, but it was an all-round combatant, serving in the ground-attack role as well as fighting at high altitude. The two-tone colour pattern is typical of the type and era.

common. By the end of the war, radar had developed to the point where visual detection was only part of the problem. As air-to-air missiles became ever more sophisticated, it was predicted that pilots would not need to sight one another to fight; aircraft would become essentially missile platforms and the dogfight would cease to exist.

Aircraft were built without guns, on the assumption that while infrared-seeking missiles were launched within visual range, electronic instrumentation was more important than the pilot's eyesight. This conclusion was faulty, and within a few years the cannon was reinstated as an essential combat system. Although electronic

Below: The P-61 Black Widow was the first of its type – a custom-designed night fighter built with radar interceptions in mind. Its primary armament of four 20mm (0.78in) cannon were intended for the rapid destruction of bombers.

150

systems aid the modern fighter pilot, he still carries out many manoeuvres by eye. Thus, making aircraft more difficult to see is still useful against both airborne and ground-fire threats. Some aircraft have a false cockpit painted on the underside of the fuselage. This is intended to create a momentary confusion about which way the aircraft is turning, which may be enough to prevent a successful attack.

Camouflage Tactics Today

Camouflage remains useful primarily against optically sighted ground fire, and thus benefits combat helicopters and low-flying attack planes. Use is also made of terrain. Apart from the obvious gambit of flying along valleys to block the enemy's line of sight, an approach can also be made with a terrain feature behind the aircraft. A camouflaged attack helicopter is very hard to see against the backdrop of a wooded hillside. This sort of terrain ambush was a regular part of NATO doctrine for countering a Soviet invasion of Europe, and remains an effective tactic today.

Camouflaging the upper surfaces of a low-flying aircraft is also useful in hiding it from fighters operating at higher altitude. Radar might tell the fighter pilot that a target is present, but if he cannot see it then attacking it will be problematic. Thus, many of the camouflage schemes that existed at the end of World War II remain useful today, at least against weapons that require the operator to see the target.

Fake Bombers and Radar Interception

The increasing use of radar by both sides made conventional camouflage less effective, but at the same time opened up new avenues for deception. Radar had proven invaluable in the Battle of Britain, enabling an effective fighter response

Friend or Foe?

Although air warfare is only a century old, certain concepts have already begun to be repeated. If one side has, or believes it will have, air superiority it tends to be concerned mainly with identification at least as much as concealment. In the modern world IFF (Identification-Friend-or-Foe) systems carry out this function automatically and, for the most part, reliably. In earlier eras this was not the case; invasion stripes, identification panels and distinctive colour schemes served the same purpose.

Where air superiority is questionable or definitely in favour of the other side, or where an aircraft is intended to penetrate hostile airspace, concealment is of paramount importance. Aircraft intended to fly high and fast, dashing through the defended zone, can dispense with optical camouflage in many cases; radar and thermal signatures are more important.

But for the low-flying strike or ground attack platform, visual detection and optically targeted attack is still as much a threat as ever. A camouflaged aircraft dashing down a valley might be heard for some distance, but visually tracking it to aim a weapon will be a problem. As in other environments, camouflage that imposes even a short delay upon gunners in aiming their weapons can save the aircraft.

to be made as enemy formations approached. Without it, reports of incoming aircraft would have been based on visual observation, which had a much shorter range.

The effectiveness of air defence radar depended upon its ability to distinguish incoming formations without 'false positive' contacts, and also upon the communications and control network that made use of the radar data. Without the latter, no amount of information was of any use. Meanwhile, if the radar produced credible but false contacts, the fighters would have been drawn out to meet non-existent threats and quite possibly have been unavailable when a real one materialized.

As the balance of the war shifted, German engineers produced increasingly advanced air defence radars and also sets that could be carried aboard a night fighter aircraft. Other nations produced radar-equipped night fighters too, but all such aircraft were subject to quite severe limitations. Early radar equipment was rather primitive and interpreting its return was something of a black art. A good radar operator used something in between technical skill and mystical intuition to pass data to his pilot or into the command and control system, and even with radar the crews of night fighters still had to visually locate a bomber stream.

The sheer numbers of bombers involved in a later-war raid meant that if a night fighter could get into the right area an interception was fairly likely. Even so, it was possible to miss a large formation on a dark night. Night fighters did exact a steady toll upon the bombers, and some means had to be found to counter them.

The Allies eventually discovered that it was possible to intercept the pulses from night fighters' radar and thus gain warning that they were approaching. Escorting aircraft, such as twin-engined Mosquito fighter-bombers, were sometimes inserted into a bomber formation to counterattack the enemy night fighters, or might loiter over night-fighter bases and ambush them as they took off. Although radar brought about these night-time combats, they were fought by eye, and effective night-time camouflage could make all the difference.

COUNTERING RADAR WITH 'WINDOW'

Another way to counter radar was to use strips of metal foil, at the time called 'window' but today known as 'chaff'. Window was only effective if the strips were cut to a length that

Right: Acoustic locators were used before radar was invented, detecting approaching aircraft at great distances by amplifying the sound of their engines. The fighter control network used in the Battle of Britain was originally created to make use of such location devices.

Above: When the decision was taken to finally begin using 'window' to confuse enemy radar, delivery was rather primitive. Bundles of window were dropped from the bomb bays of Lancasters, probably in far greater quantities than were necessary to deliver the intended result.

corresponded to the wavelength of the enemy radar. It produced a false-positive return that could blanket radar – essentially creating a smokescreen-like effect through which the enemy radar could not detect anything. This could be used to confuse the enemy in a variety of ways.

One option was to send a few aircraft into enemy territory dropping chaff, to make it look as if a large raid was in progress in that area. Having drawn enemy fighters to that region, a real attack could proceed more safely to its target elsewhere. Alternatively, window could be used to conceal a bomber formation – the enemy would be alerted that something was going on, but could not know whether the threat was a handful of decoy aircraft or a thousand-bomber raid.

This ambiguity could be used to draw enemy night fighters into an ambush or simply to force them to waste the fuel that was in increasingly short supply. Over time, it ensured that responses to bomber attacks were on a smaller scale and might be made on a piecemeal basis. The enemy could not afford to put up a concentrated response against every possible attack, which meant that sometimes a real attack was met with a paltry counter.

Window was a two-edged sword. It was withheld for some time in case the Axis reverse-engineered the concept and used it against the Allies. Eventually, with the Allies firmly on the offensive, it was decided that the benefit of reducing bomber casualties outweighed the danger of more effective enemy raids.

Window could also be used on a more local scale to confuse enemy gunnery radar and thereby defend an aircraft or formation. This is a well-proven concept in the modern world, but was a complete failure the first time it was attempted. The guns that were supposed to be confused by window had no radar, and were reliant on acoustic detection equipment. This illustrates one of the key problems with any

Chronology of Aircraft Camouflage

The thinking behind aircraft camouflage, or the lack of it, has evolved over the years but not in a straightforward manner. A changing combat environment has required a return to earlier concepts on several occasions.

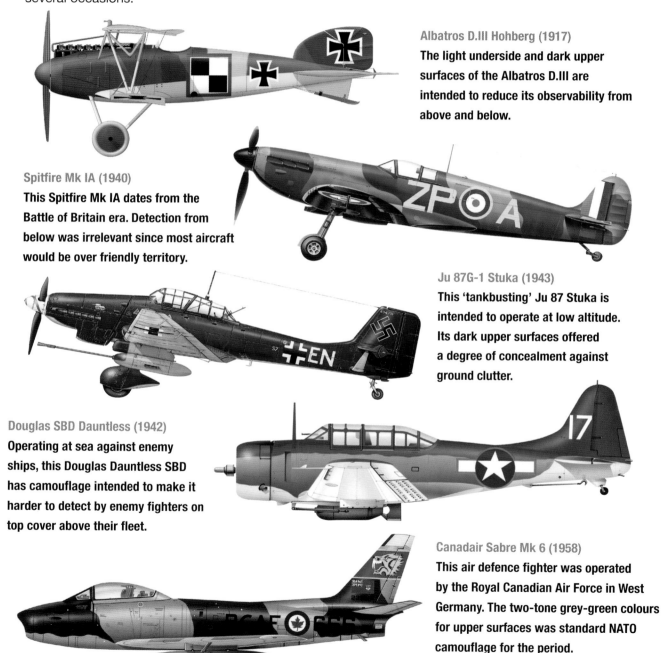

Albatros D.III Hohberg (1917)
The light underside and dark upper surfaces of the Albatros D.III are intended to reduce its observability from above and below.

Spitfire Mk IA (1940)
This Spitfire Mk IA dates from the Battle of Britain era. Detection from below was irrelevant since most aircraft would be over friendly territory.

Ju 87G-1 Stuka (1943)
This 'tankbusting' Ju 87 Stuka is intended to operate at low altitude. Its dark upper surfaces offered a degree of concealment against ground clutter.

Douglas SBD Dauntless (1942)
Operating at sea against enemy ships, this Douglas Dauntless SBD has camouflage intended to make it harder to detect by enemy fighters on top cover above their fleet.

Canadair Sabre Mk 6 (1958)
This air defence fighter was operated by the Royal Canadian Air Force in West Germany. The two-tone grey-green colours for upper surfaces was standard NATO camouflage for the period.

Lockheed C-17 Globemaster (1980)

The C-17 Globemaster is not a combat aircraft, but might come under fire when using a forward airbase. Its camouflage is geared to protecting it from ground attack.

General Dynamics F-111F (1990)

The F-111 started out as a fighter project but became a highly effective low-level strike platform. Its camouflage reflects that role during Operation Desert Storm.

Israeli F-16D Fighting Falcon (1994)

This F-16D is in Israeli colours. A sandy top side offers some concealment on the ground and when flying low as a multi-role aircraft will often do.

Rumanian Air Force MiG 21M (1995)

The MiG-21 was introduced in the Cold War era. Visual target acquisition was commonplace in engagements between aircraft, making camouflaged upper and light lower surfaces useful.

French Navy Rafale M (2004)

This Rafale M of the French Navy is a multirole fighter/strike platform for the modern era. It can operate over land or sea, but in either case the main threat is from radar and thermal detection, making optical camouflage less useful.

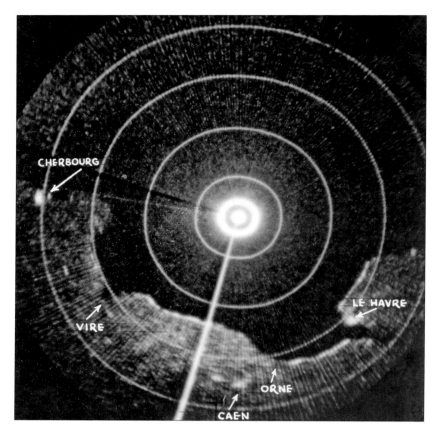

Above: A radar image of the enemy coast, taken from a US bomber during the D-Day landings. Early radar was temperamental and difficult to interpret. An effective radar operator was said to need a combination of technical skill, witchcraft and blind luck.

camouflage or deception measure – it must be appropriate to the enemy's detection system or it will fail.

FOOLING RADAR BY OTHER MEANS

Electronic means were also used to spoof enemy radars. As early as 1942, the RAF deployed aircraft equipped with a device codenamed Moonshine, which received and amplified pulses from German air defence radar. This created the impression of several aircraft flying in close formation and could draw a response away from a real raid. The use of transmitters to jam radar signals was also implemented around this time.

Measures of this sort could not conceal the fact that something was going on, but they could create doubt about whether a radar signal could be trusted. This form of camouflage may seem different from kinds that conceal an object or person, but in truth they all fulfil the same function.

The purpose of camouflage is not to deceive the enemy's eyes so much as to confuse his mind. It is there that his response is formulated, so convincing him that he cannot believe his 'eyes' (be they electronic or literal) is a highly effective form of camouflage in its own right. Confusing the radar also forced the enemy to fall back upon visual methods, against which more conventional camouflage was already in place.

Not all measures to counter the Allied bombers were as sophisticated. One method that inflicted casualties was to use deception to lead Allied crews astray. In the aftermath of a raid, there would inevitably be stragglers that had become separated from the main bomber formations. Damaged or suffering from malfunctions, or perhaps just simply lost, these lone bombers were vulnerable to fighters and also to interception of another kind.

Captured bombers were used by the Axis to trick these stragglers. A straggler might be approached by another bomber, perhaps displaying damage of its own and apparently without a functioning radio. By hand signals, waggling wings or just turning onto a new heading, the apparently friendly aircraft convinced the straggler that its crew knew the way home or at least to a safe landing spot. Crews that fell for this 'follow me home' act were led to airfields France that were under Axis control and taken prisoner.

The Allies countered these Trojan horses with disguised bombers of their own. Posing as a straggler, and usually displaying fake damage of their own, these aircraft were heavily armed in the manner of a Q-ship (see Chapter 5). Some had multiple automatic cannon positioned to fire sideways, and would open fire as soon as the crew were sure they were dealing with a turncoat aircraft. Both the deceivers and the

crews sent to counter them had to be adept at telling a truly damaged aircraft from one that was disguised with ill intent.

Stealth Technology in Air Combat

Window (or chaff) can be used as the electronic equivalent of a smokescreen to confuse enemy radar, as can active jamming. However, this is not ideal, as it will alert the enemy to the fact that something is happening even if he cannot be sure what. It also requires that the aircraft carrying jammers or deploying chaff must go in harm's way while drawing attention to itself. It is far better to avoid detection altogether. One method, discovered very soon after the invention of radar, was to fly 'under the radar', i.e. so low that the intruding aircraft was lost in the confused collection of radar returns from the ground. However, this is not always possible.

Below: One of the iconic aircraft of the Cold War era, the Harrier was designed to hide in places most aircraft could not operate from. Barns, warehouses and woodland clearings covered by camouflage nets were just some of the possible hiding places.

Above: A Bell AH-1F Cobra attack helicopter in desert camouflage during Operation Desert Storm, 1991. Helicopters can operate low enough to hide from most radar in the ground clutter, but are still vulnerable to short-range radar, thermal and optical tracking. The ability to hide behind terrain obstructions is essential to attack helicopter survivability.

It is not possible to make an aircraft invisible to radar, but it is possible to reduce its radar cross-section. This is defined as the cross-sectional area of a spherical object that would produce the same radar return as the aircraft. A large radar cross-section means that the aircraft is detected easily or at great distance. A smaller value indicates a more 'stealthy' aircraft.

Radar cross-section is influenced by many factors, including shape and construction. Metal reflects radar energy more effectively than softer materials, and sharp corners produce a greater reflection than rounded shapes. The angle at which energy is reflected also influences radar cross-section; radar sets detect the energy reflecting back from the target so one that reflects energy straight back will show up more effectively than one that scatters energy in all directions or reflects it in a direction not directly back at the receiver.

Traditional aircraft typically have a very large radar cross-section for their size since they have many angles and large metal surfaces that reflect energy. Low-observable technology and design

(typically referred to as 'stealth') attempt to reduce this cross-section by various means.

Construction is one factor. An aircraft can be at least partially built with materials that produce a lower radar return than traditional steel and aluminium, and radar return can be greatly reduced by removing sharp corners. Wings are thus often blended into the fuselage and other projections are rounded or placed at an angle that will not send enemy radar pulses straight back. Weapon mounts, engines, air intakes and other features of an aircraft are concealed as much as possible by rounding them off or placing a shroud over them.

Many 'stealth' aircraft carry their weapons in an internal bay, which greatly reduces their radar signature. Opening the bay creates extra angles and surfaces to reflect radar energy, and is thus avoided until the aircraft is ready to attack. As a result, stealth aircraft generally carry a smaller warload than traditional ones, but can deliver their weapons to targets that a more observable aircraft might not be able to reach.

RADAR-ABSORBING MATERIALS
Some materials absorb radar energy rather than reflecting it back. 'Ironball' paint contains small metal particles that vibrate when energized by radar pulses, shedding the energy locally at a low level rather than reflecting it back. A coating of such materials on the outer surfaces of an aircraft can greatly reduce its cross-section,

although the specialist materials used often require a great deal of maintenance. The B-2 bomber, for example, requires extensive support to maintain its stealth characteristics.

Other radar-absorbent materials are available, and can be combined with design features that cause radar energy to be internally reflected, essentially trapping it inside the aircraft's structure. Energy is lost with each reflection, so a signal that has bounced around inside a target will be greatly reduced in strength as well as being heavily scattered.

Active stealth systems have been trialled that attempt to cancel out enemy radar by detecting the pulse and emitting one with the exact opposite characteristics. Effectively, the two pulses add up to zero and will not be detected. However, this requires near-perfect duplication of the received pulse on an almost instantaneous basis. If the two are not perfectly synchronized there is a danger of making the aircraft more rather than less detectable.

Above: Although it was designed to have a small radar cross-section, the Lockheed SR-71 was primarily designed to defeat threats by being where it could not be attacked. Flying extremely high and fast, it could simply outpace any missile launched at it.

DISGUISING THERMAL SIGNATURE

An aircraft can also be detected using its thermal signature. This cannot be entirely eliminated, since engines are needed to propel an aircraft and these produce heat. Airflow over the fuselage can also create a heat signature at high speeds. Thermal signature can be reduced by good streamlining, which reduces frictional heating as well as permitting the aircraft to fly faster while using less engine power.

The hot exhaust from engines is the main component of thermal signature. Although some reduction is possible using lower-powered engines that generate less heat, this can only be taken so far. Thermal signature can be hidden to some extent by placing the engines where other

Left: The F-35 Lightning II, like most other modern designs, was developed with stealth in mind. Radar and thermal detection and tracking are the most serious threats, and so modern designs incorporate measures to deduce these signatures.

parts of the aircraft will conceal them. This is not always done for 'stealth-related' reasons as such; the A-10 Thunderbolt is hardly a 'stealthy' aircraft, but its engines are positioned to hide them from the thermal seekers fitted to many short-range air defence missiles.

The A-10's engines are screened by its wings and tail section from most angles – at least

Below: The F-117 Nighthawk was the first true 'stealth' aircraft into service, trading manoeuvrability and heavy weapons load for the ability to sneak into enemy airspace undetected. An F-117 could in theory ambush other aircraft, but was primarily useful as a means to suppress enemy air defences.

with reference to ground-based missiles, which are the greatest threat to an aircraft of this sort. Many 'stealth' aircraft follow this general configuration, with exhaust gases often passed over part of the aircraft's outer skin before emerging from the screened area. Although this creates heating of the area where the gases pass, it allows a great deal of cooling to occur before the exhaust becomes visible to a seeker or detector. The hot area is likewise screened by the aircraft's tail or fuselage.

This reduction of thermal and radar signature is accompanied by keeping acoustic (noise) and visual signature as low as possible. Small size, low-observable colouration and flying relatively slowly can keep the overall observability of the aircraft as low as possible. This does not translate to invisibility, but it does reduce the range at which a radar set of a given level of

power is likely to detect the aircraft. It also makes it difficult for thermal or radar-guided weapons to attack the target.

The Components of Stealth

There are two key components to stealth: reducing the level of emissions coming from an aircraft, such as sound, heat from engines and transmissions form radios or radar; and minimizing the return created when a given level of energy strikes the aircraft's structure. Stealth is only useful against electronic systems for the most part; visual detection is as likely as it has ever been.

However, it has the additional advantages of making an aircraft harder to hit with guided weapons and making decoys such as chaff or flares more effective. If a missile was already having trouble seeing its target, then the cloud

Below: The F-22 Raptor is an extremely expensive aircraft, but also an extremely capable one. Its stealthy nature can defeat many detection and tracking systems. This gives it a huge advantage in air combat even without considering its flight and weapon capabilities.

of chaff or flare that appears in its field of vision would seem a more attractive target.

Not very many years ago, the idea of a 'stealth fighter' seemed like science fiction. Today, the concepts associated with stealth are well understood and are built into all new designs to a greater or lesser degree. There is always a tradeoff between performance and observability, but there is no longer any clear dividing line between what is a stealth aircraft and what is not. Older designs are often modified when they are upgraded to make them less observable, and a degree of stealth – i.e. reduced observability – is built into most new designs as a matter of course.

By way of example, the F-22 Raptor is an air-superiority fighter, not a stealthy intruder designed to slip past radar. Yet it was designed from the outset with low observability in mind because this offered real advantages in its projected role. In just a few years, stealth technologies and concepts have matured to the point where they can be applied to almost any aircraft and, while impressive, they are also now more or less mundane.

CHAPTER 5

CAMOUFLAGE IN NAVAL WARFARE

The naval environment is quite different to that of land warfare. A ship is a very large object to hide and there is little in the way of natural cover to exploit.

A ship on the open sea is a large and often rather obvious object. However, it is tiny compared to the vast expanse of ocean around it. The curve of the Earth's surface limits the distance it is possible to see in any direction, and expedients such as putting lookouts atop a mast can only extend the range of vision so far. It is thus common for entire fleets to fail to sight one another, or for vessels to achieve surprise by approaching unseen.

In the Age of Sail (sixteenth to nineteenth centuries), it was not uncommon for a vessel's sails to be mistaken for clouds, or for ships that were actively searching for one another to miss a sighting by a matter of a few kilometres – even in good weather. Sailors have long known that it is possible to hide in a rain squall or

Opposite: HMS *Daring*, **a Type 45 destroyer. In the modern environment, making a vessel more difficult to detect and target using radar is more important than optical camouflage.**

a sheltered bay, and these techniques remain workable today.

Warships were sometimes painted to change their appearance, or their gunports concealed to make them look like a civilian vessel. The opposite approach was used to protect some civilian ships during the Age of Sail, creating a form of protective colouration by mimicking a warship. This could be achieved by painting the hull to look as if it had gunports. This was often done as a form of decoration, but also served to deter the occasional hostile act.

False Flags and Challenge and Response

Sailing under a false flag was a common ruse used by all nations as well as independents. The use of a false flag has traditionally been considered a legitimate *ruse de guerre*, providing certain rules are observed. It is acceptable to approach a target under a false flag, but opening fire without first showing the vessel's true colours constituted treachery and would invite a harsh response if the deceivers were captured. In some cases, attacks under a false flag have been considered piracy and punished accordingly.

One counter to this use of mimicry to gain an advantage is the use of codes to challenge a suspect vessel. Nautical fiction is full of examples where the characters are engaged in some form of deception and delay discovery by hoisting their response to a challenge in an unintelligible 'lubberly tangle' of signal flags. It is even possible that this really happened from time to time; certainly there have been incidents where a challenged ship responded with a confusing or an inappropriate signal.

During World War II, the destroyer HMS *Campbeltown* was packed with explosives and used to damage the dock at St Nazaire in order to prevent its use by the German battleship *Tirpitz*. The final attack was made openly, but during her approach to the target *Campbeltown* displayed a German flag and responded to challenges with the correct code letters.

This deception greatly facilitated the raid's success, which caused immense damage to the docks and prevented their use by large surface

The Pitfalls of Challenge and Response

The use of challenge and response is not infallible. After the Battle of Jutland in 1916, some German warships were able to bluff their way past the intercepting British fleet because they had observed the challenge signals and the correct response made by British vessels. In the darkness, a dimly seen ship that made the right signal was allowed to proceed. Thus, several vessels of the German High Seas Fleet were able to make it home despite being intercepted.

Above: The night action at Jutland was a confused affair in which some German vessels observed the challenge and response made by British ships that sighted one another. A few enterprising captains were able to steam boldly past the enemy, protected by a successful deception.

raiders. Although it was not possible in this case to make *Campbeltown* look like a German destroyer, appearance was less important at night than the code letters the ship flashed. Since it was inevitable that the raiding force would be spotted, deception – or at least the creation of doubt as to whether the ship approaching was friendly or not – was the best option.

Visibility rather than Concealment

Deception and concealment have not always been considered important in naval strategy. Towards the end of the nineteenth century, it was common for warships to make themselves highly visible as a means of projecting power. Naval forces were often the primary representatives of the colonial powers in that era, and were inevitably spread thinly. The appearance of vessels as smart and efficient proved an effective deterrent to aggression both by other powers and by local rebels.

The message sent by these vessels was that a smart and therefore presumably highly competent navy was in the area. Naval ostentation also assisted identification as a warship, something that is still useful today. The Straits of Malacca, among other regions, are notorious for pirates who use small boats or even helicopters to dash out from concealment along the shoreline. Pirates have been known to make mistakes and to attack naval vessels, sometimes with unfortunate consequences.

As a means of deterring piracy in general and also to prevent a mistaken attack, some warship captains operating in waters like the Straits of Malacca take measures to ensure that their ships can be seen and identified at night. One option is to pointedly illuminate the main gun and the national emblem painted on the funnel using searchlights. The message here is clear – 'take note: I am a warship'.

Painted in white, black and red, with holystoned decks and gleaming brass, the warships of the late nineteenth century were intended to be seen – and to impress. White upperworks may also have reduced the effects of the sun when operating in warmer regions. However, even in the Colonial era, there were suggestions that ships could be concealed or made more difficult targets. Visibility may be useful for deterrence but would obviously be a liability in wartime. Ideas such as countershading the vessel or using dazzle camouflage were put forward as early as the late nineteenth century but received little widespread recognition.

Camouflaging Warships

The idea of camouflaging a warship was nothing new, even if it was ignored for a time. There are accounts of galleys in the ancient world being painted shades of blue-green to conceal

them, and by the last decade of the nineteenth century, the world's major navies were experimenting with shades of grey and off-white for camouflage. The Royal Navy moved to grey in 1903, and by the time of the Great War the warships of most navies were grey.

A grey hull helped 'lose' the ship against a horizon in much the same way that grey clothing had been shown to conceal personnel at even a modest distance. However, in an era of coal-powered ships it was difficult to avoid detection. Smoke rising from a ship's stacks would be visible at a greater distance to its hull. Even after warships began to burn oil instead of coal, stack gases remained a visibility problem. As a ship approached its top speed, the amount of smoke it produced increased greatly.

This created tactical decisions for warship captains. Steaming at full speed might permit a destroyer to get into torpedo range or avoid

Below: The ships of the late nineteenth century were technical marvels of their age as well as military assets. An ironclad battleship such as HMS *Collingwood* was the public face of the British Empire; a smart and efficient ship sent a message about British military might.

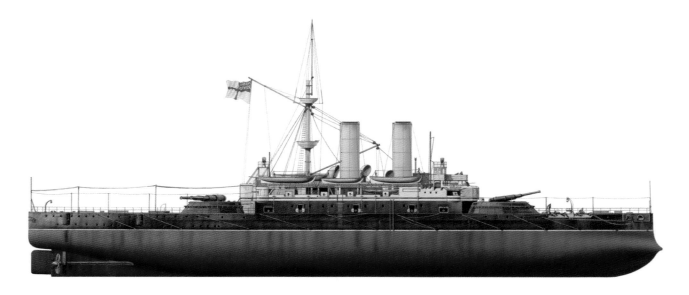

Above: HMS *Royal Oak*, launched in 1914, belonged to a new era of grey-painted, big-gun capital ships. In 1939 she was torpedoed and sunk in the supposedly secure harbour at Scapa Flow by *U-47*, demonstrating the vulnerability of battleships to surprise attack by submarines.

Below: Smokescreens rapidly became a feature of surface action, providing concealment behind which an outmatched force could slip away. Black smoke could be made by injecting oil into the ship's exhaust gases; a more sophisticated process using titanium tetrachloride produced a white smokescreen that lasted longer.

being hit if fired upon, but a slower approach was less obvious and might enable the ship to sneak closer before beginning its dash. Smoke could also obscure a ship or fleet, either deliberately as a defensive measure or due to the high-speed steaming necessary for combat.

Smoke remained a standard defensive tactic throughout both world wars, and still has some applications today. Typically, smoke was laid by fast-moving destroyers to protect a convoy or a force of more powerful vessels. Enemy gunners could not shoot accurately at what they could

not see, of course. However, a smokescreen might make it possible to break contact or to manoeuvre so that when contact was reacquired it was from an unexpected direction. Destroyers might also lay smoke then turn into it before charging back out in the hope of closing for a torpedo attack.

Against larger warships such as battleships and heavy cruisers, the advantage gained by temporary concealment could be very significant. Secondary armament might traverse quickly, but the big guns took time to come around. Vessels of a convoy that scattered behind a smokescreen had a far better chance of escape, and warships that knew where to

aim could bring their guns into action more quickly than those that had to train them on a new bearing. Smoke was thus both a defensive and offensive measure, and could also be used to defend ships in port from air attack.

Even if the enemy could see a ship, hitting it was difficult. Firing directly at any moving object is pointless unless it is travelling straight towards or away from the gun, and even then if shells are being fired in a high arc an error in estimating range will result in a miss. It was thus necessary to calculate a firing solution based on where the gunners thought the target would be when the shells arrived.

At close range, shells and torpedoes would reach the target in a fairly short time, during which the target would not move or change course very much. At longer ranges, the target had more time to turn or change speed, and more time for these manoeuvres to take effect. Any error in calculating the range or heading of the target would be magnified by the distance from firer to target.

Below: HMS _Erebus_ supported the Allied landings in Sicily in July 1943. Although they were designed to outrange shore-based guns it was not always possible to remain out of reach. A dazzle camouflage pattern that made it difficult to predict the ship's future location by observing her speed and heading provided effective protection from counter-battery fire.

Above: Some Royal Navy camouflage schemes were intended to conceal or create confusion about the identity of a ship. The distinctive layout of HMS *Rodney* and her sister *Nelson* made this difficult, but dazzle camouflage could still make estimating her course and speed more of a challenge.

The Tactic of Dazzle Camouflage

It was possible to make the already difficult task of putting shells into a ship's projected future position that much harder by changing heading even a little, and the use of 'dazzle' camouflage and similar methods added another layer of difficulty. British experiments early in the Great War were based on the work of Thayer and Kerr, and seemed promising. They were derailed by largely political concerns, however, and later work was undertaken under the auspices of Norman Wilkinson.

Wilkinson's primary concern was to protect merchant shipping from U-boat attack. German submarines proved extremely effective once unrestricted warfare was permitted, and imposed heavy losses both on merchant ships and the much-needed goods they carried. At the outset of the Great War there was little that could be done to counter U-boats; submarine tracking was in its infancy and there were no anti-submarine weapons. If one could be caught on the surface it might be shelled or rammed, but if it succeeded in diving it was fairly safe. That situation changed rapidly with the

development of depth charges, anti-submarine rocket launchers and tracking methods including hydrophones and what would become known as sonar (shortened from the term 'sound navigation and ranging').

However, even once submarines could be effectively attacked when underwater it was still useful to reduce the chances of a torpedo hit. Dazzle camouflage made it difficult to estimate speed and heading, which could also be done by painting a false bow wave on the vessel. Bow wave height relative to the vessel's size was an indicator of speed, so disguising this could throw off the enemy's aim by a larger margin.

Dazzle camouflage was useful not only as the enemy calculated his firing solution, but could make an attack impossible by causing the submarine commander to position his vessel wrongly. Unlike shells and missiles, torpedoes travel only a little faster than a ship. They will take longer to reach a vessel moving away from the firer, increasing the margin for error even if they do not run out of fuel during a long stern chase.

In order to obtain a reasonable chance of a hit, a U-boat commander had to position his vessel ahead of the target's projected position. Whether this was accomplished by racing on the surface or sneaking into position underwater, if the target's course was incorrectly estimated the submarine might find itself out of position and unable to launch with any chance of success.

Dazzle paintwork could also defend a vessel against air attack with bombs or torpedoes. An aircrew had only a few seconds to line up their attack and were usually under fire at the time. Hitting a moving target, even one as large as a ship, was not easy under those conditions. Dazzle paintwork could cause confusion about which way a vessel was turning and cause an attack to over- or undershoot, or to miss entirely. This was particularly true of high-level attacks where the margin for error was greater.

Testimony from those who attempted to attack dazzle-painted ships suggests that it was highly effective in confusing the observer about the type and even number of ships present. There is also evidence that even when these ships were successfully attacked, more hits were of a marginal nature than on vessels that were not dazzle-painted. However, there is no solid consensus as to the effectiveness of dazzle camouflage, nor which types were most useful.

Ship Camouflage in World War II

Dazzle camouflage was deemed sufficiently effective to be employed in both World Wars by the British and US navies. German ships of the Great War era did not make much use of camouflage, perhaps because the threat of submarine attack was much lower, but camouflage did appear for the invasion of Norway in 1940.

Opposite, above: After suffering extremely heavy damage in November 1940, HMS *Javelin* spent 1941 under repair, returning to service in March 1942 to patrol duties in the Mediterranean.

Opposite, lower: USS *Calhoun* was a World War I-era 'four-stacker' destroyer brought out of retirement for service in World War II. During the fighting for Guadalcanal *Calhoun* served as a fast supply and troop transport. She was sunk off Guadalcanal by air attack in August 1942.

The patterns used took the form of diagonal stripes for the most part, and were intended to protect vessels in port or close to the coast. Air attack was a significant hazard for these ships, and their camouflage was probably aimed at countering this threat. Raiders intended for operations in open seas used a plain grey colour scheme instead.

At the outbreak of World War II, the Royal Navy reimplemented camouflage on a largely unofficial and uncoordinated basis. Measures were designed to counter the threats deemed most likely at the time. Royal Navy vessels were protected against the possibility of air attack by camouflage schemes matching the local conditions of their home port. These were mainly disruptive patterns including dazzle schemes, and may have been intended to confuse reconnaissance pilots about what kind of ships were in port as much as to defend against attack. Similar attempts were made later in the war to disguise the identity of capital ships rather than to camouflage them as such.

By late 1940, these early camouflage schemes had been largely supplanted by regulation grey, which varied in shade according to the vessel's intended area of operations. There were exceptions, however. Some Royal Navy vessels operating in home waters used a colour scheme named Mountbatten Pink after the commander of the flotilla that first used it. This pinkish-grey colour was thought to make ships harder to see in poor light conditions than standard grey, and was adopted on a limited basis. It remained controversial, with many observers concluding that it was no better than standard grey.

ROYAL NAVY CAMOUFLAGE

The Royal Navy did not make much of an organized attempt to implement camouflage until late 1940, and even then the schemes

developed by the newly formed camouflage section were not put into operation for nearly two years. Unsurprisingly perhaps, Royal Navy camouflage used blue and green as well as grey for most of its camouflage.

One of the most important sea areas as far as the Royal Navy was concerned was the Western Approaches, the area immediately to the west of the British Isles. No matter where the vessels came from or were headed, ships entering or leaving British ports had to pass through this area. A camouflage scheme geared to the needs of vessels moving through this area was implemented by the Admiralty.

The Western Approaches camouflage scheme was largely the work of Peter Scott, son of the famous Antarctic explorer who was serving

Above: The light cruiser HMS *Glasgow* served for a time in the Far East but spent much of her World War II service in the cold, dark waters of the North Sea and the Arctic convoy routes.

aboard the destroyer HMS *Broke*. In 1940, *Broke* was given an experimental camouflage pattern that might have worked a little too well – she was involved in a collision with another vessel whose captain said he had not seen the destroyer.

Western Approaches Camouflage was implemented in 1941 and was primarily concerned with toning down the appearance of a ship's superstructure to make it less visible at a distance. A mix of irregular polygonal shapes of different colours and countershading to remove distinct edges was deemed most effective, although variants continued to appear throughout the war and US vessels used their own variation on the theme.

Further experimentation was led by a section of the Naval Research Laboratory, which used model ships painted in various camouflage

Below: USS *Nevada* was one of the battleships attacked at their moorings in Pearl Harbor on 7th December 1941, which illustrated the vulnerability of warships at anchor to air attack. *Nevada* was the only capital ship able to get under way, but this did not save her from repeated hits.

schemes and a theatrical light rig to simulate different conditions against various backdrops. Naval camouflage remained an emerging science, however, and conclusions drawn from research were not always borne out in reality. The increasing use of radar at sea both for detection and gunlaying made camouflage less useful even as research increased the body of knowledge upon which it was based.

US NAVY CAMOUFLAGE

The US Navy had experimented with camouflage from before the beginning of the 20th century, and from 1935 onwards work was undertaken at the Naval Research Laboratory into reducing the visibility of warships on the open sea. A more formal camouflage doctrine emerged from this work than was the case with British ships, with captains given little leeway regarding implementation of camouflage patterns.

As with other nations, the US Navy sought to meet two goals with its camouflage schemes:

Above: USS *Indiana* came under heavy air attack at the Battle of the Philippine Sea in 1944, and was attacked by kamikaze aircraft off Okinawa, but the heaviest damage she suffered was in a night-time collision with USS *Washington* whilst both ships were blacked-out to protect them from enemy attack.

to reduce visibility by making vessels fade into the horizon, and to create ambiguity about a sighted vessel's identity and heading. A series of numbered measures emerged from this experimentation, starting with Measure 1, which was a set of changes to the existing grey colour schemes. This might be combined with Measure 5, which required adding a false bow wave to one of the other camouflage schemes.

Some measures were specific to certain classes of vessel, such as painting the silhouette of one class of ship on another, whereas others were variants on existing measures. Measure 11 began life as Measure 1A, a variant on Measure 1 using blue rather than grey. Measure 21

Right: The German battleship *Bismarck*, wearing a subtle camouflage system designed to confuse enemy gunners. Changes in colouration towards the ends of the ship, combined with the obvious stripes, make it hard to determine where the bow and stern of the ship are, and thus to estimate range and heading.

likewise was first trialled as 1C, using a different shade of blue. The most enduring of these concepts was Measure 9, which was applied only to submarines. The Measure 9 all-over dull black colour remains standard today.

Shortly before the US entered World War II, a set of revised measures was implemented, although not all vessels were able to obtain the necessary colours. Measures 11 and 12 used a primarily sea blue colour, with superstructures painted ocean grey and higher structures in haze grey under Measure 12. Measure 12 was found to be ineffective against aerial observation in the Pacific theatre and was replaced by a modified version or a reversion to Measure 11.

Measure 13, all-over haze grey, was little used during the war, although it has become a common warship colour since. Dazzle patterns became common from 1942, in many cases based on British experience, and were further revised with reference to US aviators' observations. In the Pacific theatre, the primary threat to Allied vessels was detection and attack by aircraft, so reducing visibility from above was an important consideration. Rather than being lost against a hazy horizon, a ship might well be outlined against a blue sea, making various shades of blue a good camouflage choice.

AXIS NAVY CAMOUFLAGE

For Allied vessels operating in the Atlantic, submarine and surface attack was the main threat, so camouflage patterns designed to

protect against these possibilities were the most logical choice. The German navy, on the other hand, did not have such a large body of experience to work from and seems to have implemented camouflage (where it was used at all) on a disjointed basis. As already noted, some ships were given camouflage for the invasion of Norway, but schemes were changed quite frequently as the war went on.

Smaller German vessels were often painted pale grey, and larger ones typically had false bows and sterns on their flanks to confuse an observer about the size and heading of the vessel. In some cases, the ends of the ship were painted in paler colours than the main hull to make the areas beyond the false bow less obvious. However, camouflage does not seem to have been a priority for many ships. *Bismarck* was given dazzle camouflage when deployed to Norway, but by the time it broke out into

the Atlantic to go raiding it was painted in plain grey.

Scharnhorst was also camouflaged for part of its career but later was given colours intended to make it more rather than less obvious. With huge Swastikas on the deck at bow and stern, and yellow or red turret tops, the ship was painted for recognition by aircraft rather than concealment. The assumption was presumably that when operating under friendly air cover the danger from a mistaken attack was greater than that of a strike by the enemy. Vessels intending to operate away from air cover were less ostentatiously decorated.

Italian warships were given dazzle camouflage but were also concerned with recognition by friendly forces. Operating in the Mediterranean, Italian ships were usually within range of friendly air cover, so identification was more of a concern than concealment. Italian ships thus

often carried patterns of stripes on their deck to aid in identification when seen from above.

Similarly, the Imperial Japanese Navy (IJN) did not see much need for camouflage at the outset of the war. Some attempt was made to protect aircraft carriers from air attack by using dazzle-painted decks, but other than this largely ineffective measure, camouflage was not implemented on anything but a local level until late 1944.

By this time the IJN was operating at a heavy disadvantage in terms of air power and suffering heavy losses from air attack. Various attempts were made at camouflage, but there was no coherent body of knowledge and the measures that were reimplemented were not effective.

During the Battle of the Atlantic, the Canadian navy conducted experiments in counter-illumination, attempting to match local light levels by shining diffuse lights onto the hull and superstructure. The lights were mounted on improvised supports and in early trials were very fragile, but over time a more robust lighting rig was developed that could survive the rigours of sea service.

By 1943, the system was sufficiently well developed to permit operational use, and was determined to greatly reduce the observability of the vessel. However, the lights were still fragile and responded slowly to changes in local lighting conditions. An attempt to use counterillumination to make a warship seem like a non-threatening vessel may have been a partial success – the target submarine ignored the approaching warship until alerted by other means – but the system as a whole was too

delicate for large-scale use. Nevertheless, the Canadian experiments advanced the science of camouflage and were influential on an aircraft-based system developed by the US Navy.

Disguising Ships

In some cases, it was possible to disguise a vessel rather than conceal it. This might be done to get through a blockade or to avoid attack by seeming to be a neutral vessel. Sea trade and the maritime movement of goods played an important part in both World Wars, with German submarines posing a grave threat to Britain's overseas supply lines and the Allies implementing a crippling blockade of German ports.

One answer to the blockade was to try to slip merchant ships past the patrols using a combination of speed, stealth and deception. False flags were an option, as was diverting into neutral waters where the other side had no authority to stop and search suspect vessels. As events such as the Altmark Incident showed, the Royal Navy was willing to ignore international

Below: The Italian battleship *Vittorio Veneto* tended to operate close to home, under friendly air cover. Thus whilst she was camouflaged against surface gunfire, air attack was considered less of a threat. *Vittorio Veneto* was one of the ships attacked in Taranto harbour by British Swordfish aircraft, but escaped without damage.

law if a suspect vessel also appeared to be doing so. Since sailing under a false flag or taking refuge in someone else's territorial waters did not necessarily offer protection from interception, the only real answer was to be fast, stealthy and sneaky.

BLOCKADE RUNNERS AND COMMERCE RAIDERS

Blockade runners managed to get in and out of German ports throughout the war – some on several occasions. Small, fast ships were favoured as blockade runners as they could move through a patrolled area quickly but were hard to spot from a distance. The chance of a patrolling vessel's radius of vision coinciding

Below: The German blockade runner *Altmark* attempted to evade interception by hiding in Norwegian fjords and remaining in the territorial waters of then-neutral Norway. She was intercepted by Royal Navy destroyer HMS *Cossack* in the controversial '*Altmark* Incident', which may have contributed to Hitler's decision to invade Norway.

with a vessel's location decreased rapidly the more quickly it was moving.

The sort of vessels that made good blockade runners were also suitable for conversion into commerce raiders. Designated 'auxiliary cruisers' or 'Hilfskreuzers', these vessels were fragile and could not stand up to the armament of a real warship, but they were not intended to. Often converted from fast vessels such as fruit carriers, these raiders were designed to slip out through the blockade and attack Allied shipping.

Commerce raiding has traditionally been the preserve of the weaker naval power in a major war, but it is nevertheless a potent weapon. Not only are merchant ships and their cargoes lost, but the naval vessels sent to hunt a raider must be pulled away from duties elsewhere. Vessels hunting raiders were not protecting convoys in the Atlantic or the Arctic, nor were they available to fight the powerful Italian navy in the Mediterranean.

Some raiders even managed to sink major warships, though any fight between a lightly

Above: The *Hilfskreuzer Atlantis* was spectacularly successful, mainly due to her frequent changes of identity and careful selection of targets. At times pretending to be an innocent merchant ship, at others boldly steaming along under a false flag, *Atlantis* evaded interception for many months despite German propaganda more or less telling the Allies where she was operating.

armed converted freighter and a real warship was likely to be one-sided. The mutual sinking of the raider *Kormoran* and the Australian light cruiser HMAS *Sydney* remains shrouded in mystery. It is likely that *Kormoran* lured its opponent in close by creating doubt about its identity or even by completely deceiving the Australian ship's officers. It is doubtful that *Kormoran* chose to engage *Sydney*; raiders were intended to strike at many soft targets such as merchantmen rather than expending themselves in a near-suicidal attack on a warship.

Successful commerce raiders did not simply sail around looking for a target. Their captains were judicious in how and when to make an attack, selecting lone merchant ships and

striking by surprise. A raider was far more likely to survive if the target did not get a distress call off at all. One way to avoid this was to approach without arousing suspicion and then to force a surrender under the suddenly revealed guns of the raider. This was also a good way to avoid loss of life – a crew could be ordered into the lifeboats or taken prisoner before their ship was sunk. It also conserved ammunition.

THE CHANGING IDENTITY OF *ATLANTIS*

Many raiders assumed the identity of real ships, often vessels belonging to neutral nations. Usually a ship of similar design was chosen, but it was not uncommon to build a false funnel or to remove one in order to give the ship an entirely different appearance. By way of example, the German Hilfskreuzer *Atlantis* assumed the identity of a Russian naval auxiliary for its breakout into the Atlantic in early 1940.

The deception involved repainting the ship and ensuring that one of its scouting floatplanes was clearly visible to observers. It, naturally, was painted as a Soviet aircraft. It proved difficult to create a convincing name to be emblazoned on the side of the ship, so the crew copied the only piece of Cyrillic writing they could find. It thus sailed under the enchanting name *Keep Clear of the Propellers*.

Atlantis was not spotted by any Russian speakers, and managed to get out into the Atlantic. Later, it assumed the identity of a Japanese merchantman (Japan was at that time not at war with the Allies) and later a Dutch freighter. Its task was not made any easier by vainglorious trumpetings on the German radio about the successes scored by a commerce raider, which more or less gave away its position, nor by the fact that a vessel it attacked burned furiously and refused to sink, increasing the risk of attracting naval patrols. The vessel whose identity *Atlantis* had stolen was then reported on

Below: Among the disguises adopted by the raider *Pinguin* were a Russian freighter and later a Greek merchant ship. At one point *Pinguin* used a seaplane disguised as an RAF aircraft to drop messages to a target vessel, ordering it to a rendezvous that was ostensibly with an Allied vessel.

the radio as being sunk, forcing another change of disguise.

Atlantis took several ships before discovering aboard one of its prizes a newspaper that correctly reported its identity. This prompted another change of appearance and the creation of two false masts. It also benefited from a spectacular piece of good luck when conducting a refuelling at sea with one of its captures. Another ship of the same line, seeing two vessels close together with boats in the water between them, assumed one was in trouble and raced up to assist. It ended up another prize of *Atlantis* for its trouble.

Atlantis at one point encountered its fellow raider *Pinguin*. With both ships disguised, a clash might have occurred had *Pinguin's* captain not suspected that *Atlantis* might be an Allied armed merchant cruiser and avoided contact. Similarly, on another occasion, *Atlantis* became suspicious of what had seemed like an inviting target and broke off its approach in case it was being lured into a trap.

Atlantis later disguised itself as an Allied armed merchantman, by modifying its main gun to look more like an Allied design and ensuring

Battleship Camouflage, 1900–1945

Naval technology advanced at an incredible pace towards the end of
the nineteenth and into the twentieth century. Many of the ships that
fought in both World Wars were based upon experimental concepts.

USS *Iowa* (1897)
**Commissioned in 1897, USS *Iowa*
was a huge improvement over the
preceding class of coastal battleships,
but was soon outdated herself.**

Mikasa (1902)
**Flagship of the Japanese
fleet at the decisive Battle
of Tsushima Strait in 1903,
Mikasa was a potent force
at sea but, like all pre-
dreadnoughts, she was made
obsolete by the big-gun
capital ship.**

Schleswig-Holstein (1908)
**One of the last generation of pre-
dreadnoughts, *Schleswig-Holstein*
was obsolescent even when she was
built. Nevertheless, she remained
in service until 1944 when she was
sunk by air attack.**

HMS *Queen Elizabeth* (1913)

The super-dreadnoughts of the *Queen Elizabeth* class were the first capital ships to mount 15-inch guns. They were vulnerable to submarine attack, however; HMS *Barham* was lost this way.

Deutschland (1933)

Another attempt to get around the limitations of the Washington Treaty, the heavy cruiser *Deutschland* received several upgrades to her anti-aircraft armament.

Vittorio Veneto (1940)

Italian battleship *Vittorio Veneto* was temporarily immobilised by air attack at the Battle of Cape Matapan, but escaped before surface ships could get into range.

USS *Indiana* (1942)

USS *Indiana* was launched at a time when the big-gun ship was being supplanted by the aircraft carrier. The changed strategic situation was not yet apparent, but the success of naval air power would soon make it clear.

Above: HMS *Fidelity* was a 'special service ship', disguised as a neutral merchant vessel to carry commando raiding parties. Many special service ships acted as submarine decoys, sometimes known as Q-ships or Trap-ships. From 1942, *Fidelity* was armed with four concealed 4-inch (100mm) guns and four torpedo tubes.

that it was highly visible. This worked very well; on one occasion *Atlantis* managed to put a boarding party aboard a prize before they realized it was not a British auxiliary cruiser, capturing the vessel without resistance. On another, an officer went aboard a potential prize dressed in Royal Navy coat and hat, and with an armed boarding party hidden in his boat.

The ruse was dramatically revealed when he threw away his British hat and coat, put the German hat he had brought upon his head, and declared the target vessel his prize. This was emphasized by taking a rifle from one of the vessel's stunned crew and throwing it overboard. The vessel's adventures continued until November 1942, when it was finally sunk by the British heavy cruiser HMS *Devonshire*. When it was caught, *Atlantis* was refuelling a U-boat and had no chance to escape or outfight a proper warship.

The last action of *Atlantis* was itself a piece of deception, trying to lure *Devonshire* into a position where it might be torpedoed by the U-boat. *Devonshire's* captain had heard of other warships lured close to raiders and badly damaged as a result, and was highly cautious. Once sure that he had cornered a commerce raider, he stood off and shelled it until it sank.

The raiding cruise of *Atlantis* was the longest of any German commerce raider. In 622 days, it sank 22 ships and captured six more. Its success was due to a combination of cunning and caution, with its many changes of identity contributing to its longevity. Although not making use of camouflage in the sense of concealment, *Atlantis* demonstrated that barefaced mimicry could be just as effective. Its deceptions incorporated elements from the largest scale to the smallest – from fake funnels and a repainting of the entire ship to false uniforms and other small details. The tales of other successful raiders are similarly filled with clever deception, often implemented with the most basic of materials.

THE TRICKERY OF Q-SHIPS

The submarine is commonly associated with torpedo attacks, but a submersible can only carry so many torpedoes. When they are expended it must either return to port – a hazardous undertaking for a U-boat operating in the Atlantic or even further afield – or rendezvous with a supply vessel. This is not a safe undertaking, either.

Thus, even when not restricted from making torpedo attacks without warning, submarines often used their deck guns to attack targets that would not offer significant resistance. As with surface raiders, this sometimes allowed the target crew to escape in their lifeboats and thus avoided unnecessary loss of life. Naval personnel, even those assigned to U-boats, generally felt protective towards unarmed merchant crews and rarely had any relish for sinking their ships. Thus, a significant proportion of submarine attacks in the World Wars were made on the surface, and it was not uncommon for a submarine to surface in order to use its guns to finish off a torpedoed merchantman. This created an opportunity to ambush submarines using armed vessels disguised as ordinary merchant ships.

These vessels were given a set of secret registries all beginning with Q, thus creating a nickname for all vessels that operated in this fashion. Disguising a Q-ship as a hopeless freighter was not entirely similar to creating a disguised commerce raider, but followed similar general principles. It was rarely necessary to make the Q-ship look like a specific vessel; all that was necessary was to conceal its nature and at least some of its armament. Many merchant ships were given a gun or two for self-defence, so a completely unarmed vessel sailing alone was likely to arouse more suspicion than one that had a token armament.

The key to creating a convincing Q-ship was to make the vessel look 'plausible'. A submarine commander observing it through his periscope had to be convinced he was looking at a ship that was not too dangerous to attack but also not so defenceless as to be obviously a trap. Since the crew could not know whether they were under observation or not, their deceptive measures had to be constant and habitual, and the vessel's own disguise must not be allowed to slip.

Upon occasion, a torpedoed Q-ship remained stubbornly afloat and tempted its attacker to surface before finally unveiling its guns and counterattacking. The decision to keep the guns and their crews hidden aboard a burning and slowly sinking vessel was difficult, but such choices were part of being a successful Q-ship crew.

The Deceptions of Submarines

For their part, submarines also engaged in a number of deceptive behaviours. Submarines could of course hide underwater, but this did not make detection impossible. Generally submarines were painted grey or black, but experiments were carried out with blues and greens for service in very clear waters such as the Mediterranean. Paintwork whose colour could be modified was also trialled.

Inventive Measures

Some crews (of both Q-ships and raiders) dressed some personnel up as women, and many Q-ships had a 'panic party' whose job was to make a big performance of getting into lifeboats and rowing frantically away from their ship. This sort of activity was intended to help convince an enemy commander that he really was dealing with a merchant ship. Buoyant materials were sometimes carried rather than cargo, in the hope that these would make the vessel more survivable if damaged in combat.

Above: The Italian submarine *Brin* operated in the Atlantic and the Mediterranean. The clear, shallow waters of the latter made submarines easy to spot from the air, even when submerged. Experiments in submarine camouflage included the use of greys, blues and greens as well as some patterns.

For the most part, submarines relied on being small and low to the water when on the surface. Running on the surface was necessary for high speed – although a bow wave might be spotted at distances where the conning tower and hull were virtually invisible – and to recharge batteries until the invention of the snorkel. Battery life was strictly limited and speeds were slow underwater, so unless a commander got lucky and found himself ahead of a ship or convoy he would have to dash into position for his attack using his superior surface speed.

Below: *U-553* operated in the Atlantic Ocean. Like similar vessels of the era, she was not a true submarine but might better be considered a torpedo boat that could submerge to hide. The dash to get ahead of a convoy was a particularly hazardous time as the U-boat had to transit at high speed on the surface.

Many commanders preferred to make torpedo attacks on the surface, and some used their vessel's low profile to sneak inside a convoy's defended perimeter before attacking. Usually the escorts would assume that an attack came from outside the convoy and spread out, and lookouts also tended to look outward rather than between the lines of merchant ships. This gave the submarine a chance to make additional attacks at close range before diving and slipping away. It required a steady nerve and a certain amount of cheek, not to mention a great deal of skill to predict the convoy's path.

Submarines sometimes used other deceptive measures, such as deliberately discharging oil and debris in the hope that enemy destroyers would presume the boat sunk. At least one U-boat disguised itself as a surface ship to avoid pursuit. This was *U-977*, whose crew decided to make the long passage to Argentina rather than return to their home port as ordered upon Germany's surrender in 1945.

U-977 made a record-breaking 66-day underwater passage using her snorkel apparatus to obtain air for the crew and the diesel engines, but once well into the Atlantic she proceeded

on the surface. Since submarines that had not complied with the surrender order were subject to attack, *U-977* was disguised by the creation of a dummy funnel, in which a small fire was lit to create the illusion of smoke. From a distance, and lacking much in the way of a frame of reference to indicate it was far too low in the water to be a surface vessel, the submarine might pass for a small merchant ship.

U-977 managed to reach Argentina and surrender to the authorities there, giving rise to all manner of conspiracy theories that it had carried senior Nazi officials into exile. This is impossible; it was off the Norwegian coast at the time of the surrender and could not have taken on personnel from elsewhere. However, its passage to Argentina stands as both an incredible feat of endurance – snorkelling for two months must have been a horrible experience for the crew – and a triumph of improvised camouflage that carried the vessel safely through the sea lanes.

Underwater Detection

Modern submarines spend very little time on the surface, as opposed to those of the two World Wars, which were essentially submersible torpedo

Above: A U-boat is attacked by Allied aircraft. A U-boat commander had a choice between relatively high speed on the surface or creeping along underwater until his batteries ran out, at which point he would have to surface. A U-boat caught on the surface was very vulnerable to air attack, but might escape observation due to its small size.

boats. A wartime submarine could submerge to hide and might lie on a shallow seabed for an extended period, but its captain had to be concerned with detectability when on the surface. This is no longer the case, and in most cases considerations like colour or camouflage patterns are irrelevant for submarines.

Visual detection of underwater objects is possible only down to quite shallow depths, although in very clear water an observer with a high vantage point such as aboard an aircraft can often make out the shape of a submarine against the seabed. This is only the case in some areas, so some other means of detection and tracking must be used.

Sound travels well through water, making it the detection and tracking system of choice. Active sonar is the equivalent of radar for underwater use, sending out pulses of sound and analyzing the reflections. The drawback with

Above: A multi-function towed array (MFTA) sonar can be fitted to most surface vessels without extensive dockyard work, and most warships have at least some anti-submarine capability. Exercises such as this one aboard USS *Farragut* have shown that detecting the new generation of attack submarines is extremely difficult.

active emissions of this sort is that they can be detected at a much greater distance than they serve to detect other objects. Active sonar is, however, very useful in localizing a contact.

PASSIVE SONAR

Passive sonar is a matter of listening for the sounds emitted by a contact; it requires no active emissions, so does not give away the position of the sonar-using vessel. A certain amount of noise is inevitable in any vessel, especially where large propulsion machinery is in use. Underwater stealth, then, is not so much about hiding from sight as reducing the vessel's acoustic signature and its sonar return.

Measures such as slowing down engines and making sure crew members do not drop anything on the deck can go a long way towards reducing acoustic signature, as can mounting machinery on 'rafts' within the vessel such that the vibrations created by machinery are absorbed by buffers before they are transmitted to the hull. These measures make a submarine or other vessel much harder to detect using passive measures.

Water flow over the hull and especially propellers creates noise, and at high speeds can result in cavitation. Cavitation occurs mainly around propeller blades, and is caused by the formation of bubbles that then collapse. Although hardly noisy by the standards of human hearing, cavitation can be detected at long distances by sensitive sonar equipment. One solution is to use a large, slowly rotating screw instead of a fast-moving smaller one. Cavitation is also decreased by depth, so a submarine can run faster at greater depth without cavitating.

Above: The sonar room aboard USS *Normandy* maintains a constant watch for underwater contacts. The only effective defence against a submarine is to detect it before it can launch weapons, and 'break the kill chain' by attacking first.

Alternative propulsion systems such as waterjets seek to eliminate cavitation at all speeds and also to reduce the number of flat surfaces and sharp corners that cause noisy water flow over the hull. Active sonar return is also reduced by not having a large-bladed screw on the back of a submarine. Another measure used to reduce active sonar return is to clad the hull with anechoic tiles. These absorb both the submarine's self-noise and the sonar energy emitted by an active searcher.

ACTIVE SONAR

Active sonar can be confused in two other ways. One is to hide among seabed clutter, which creates a confusing and chaotic sonar return in

which a submarine can be lost. The other is to make use of the properties of water itself.

In open water, temperature layers are commonly encountered, often with fairly large temperature differences on each side of an inversion layer. Known as the thermocline, or simply 'the layer', this is extremely useful to submariners and those that hunt them. A thermocline will reflect sonar energy in much the same manner as light can be refracted where air and water meet. This can distort a sonar pulse to the point where it bounces back up to the surface rather than penetrating deeper into water.

A submarine on the other side of 'the layer' to a searching sonar operator is far less likely to be detected than one that is on the same side. Knowing the temperature conditions and the likely position of the layer in any given area of water is a vital skill in submarine and anti-submarine warfare. There are additional considerations too, as the distortion due to the thermocline can cause convergence zones where

Opposite: Sonar operations are complex, since they rely on the behaviour of sound waves in a complex environment. Changes in water temperature or salinity can alter the propagation of sound waves, occasionally permitting a contact at great range and more often making the sonar operator's task very difficult indeed.

sounds from quite distant sources are picked up strongly. This can permit a fleeting contact at great distance as a submarine moves through a convergence zone, alerting hostiles to the fact that something is amiss.

To the uninitiated, it might seem that there is nowhere and no way to hide in open water, but this is far from the case. For the submariner, camouflage has little to do with visual contact. It is a matter of reducing the amount of sound the vessel makes and understanding how to make use of the natural conditions in water.

Coastal Camouflage

Ships in port are highly vulnerable to air attack. The first to be sunk in this manner was the light cruiser *Königsberg*, in 1940, and since then not even heavily armoured battleships have proven immune to bombing. Powerful air defences and fighter patrols can do so much, but without the ability to manouevre, a warship is a big target.

Camouflage offers a measure of defence against air attack, especially when combined with anti-aircraft fire or defensive air power. A pilot who has the leisure to take a good look may be able to pick out a camouflaged ship and perhaps even attack the optimum point on it;

Below: The German cruiser *Königsberg* was the first major warship to be sunk by air attack, in April 1940. Previously, it was not known for sure whether aircraft could significantly harm a warship.

one who is trying to avoid being shot down has a more difficult task and may not even be able to find the target.

The problems inherent in camouflaging a vessel in port are not inconsiderable. A ship is a large object and there will be strong clues to where it must be. Ships in port tend to lie along a quayside where the land meets the water; looking at such points will guide the observer to a camouflaged ship. Thus it is useful not just to camouflage the ship but also any landmarks that might serve to guide attackers to it.

Painting decks to match the colours of the buildings and other structures of the port can help, but for the most part netting offers the best camouflage. Netting cannot merely be strung over the ship, since this will create a ship-shaped outline that is also obvious. Instead, netting must blend the ship with the shore and soften its distinctive outlines.

Smoke is a useful addition to such camouflage measures. Even if the target cannot be completely obscured it may be possible to deprive the observer of continuous vision, making it hard to pick out the target, or to hide parts of it and similarly prevent the eye from building a picture that adds up to a definite location. However, if smoke only covers the target, then attackers can aim their weapons into it with a reasonable chance of success. A smokescreen needs to be large enough to cover an area much larger than the ship; again, it will be no use if there are obvious clues such as a straight quayside to follow into the smoke.

In short, when camouflaging a vessel in port it is necessary to obscure the whole area, including all the places where a ship might be in order to prevent the enemy from simply aiming at where the vessel must surely be even if they cannot see it. An alternative is to disguise the

Below: This antique Allied landing ship stands on a Normandy beach, testament to the amphibious assault of 6th June 1944. It is painted in a black and sand-brown two-tone – appropriate colours for the night crossing of the English Channel and morning landings.

Above: During the Vietnam War, extensive riverine operations were undertaken. Patrol boats were at constant risk of attack by forces concealed in the riverbank vegetation, but could be partially hidden by remaining close to one bank. Observers on the far side might lose sight of the boat against the backdrop of trees.

vessel so that its identity is not clear. It may be possible to hide a high-value warship among freighters or even wrecks if the vessels are all given a similar general appearance.

For vessels intended to operate close to the shore or on rivers, camouflage paint schemes offer many advantages. Engagement ranges tend to be quite short in this environment, and many weapons are manually aimed. Camouflage not only assists in avoiding detection, perhaps permitting a strike by surprise, but can also confuse the aim of enemy gunners.

Coastal and riverine combatants tend to use camouflage very similar to that employed by land forces in the same theatre, often with the addition of more grey and blue tones. Traditionally, these vessels have tended to be relatively small, ranging

from World War II-era PT (patrol torpedo) boats to US Coast Guard cutters deployed for operations in the coastal waterways of Vietnam. However, increasingly, major naval forces are tending to operate in the littoral rather than the open ocean.

This move towards 'brown water' operations (as opposed to 'blue water', or open ocean) has led to changing requirements. New warships tend to have an inbuilt land-attack capability and are designed with littoral operations much more in mind than in the past. Open-water capability cannot be sacrificed, but in the modern world naval assets must be able to support land forces or to project power inland. This necessitates going close inshore at least some of the time.

Stealth Ships

The need to operate close inshore deprives naval forces of one of their key advantages – the ability to be almost anywhere in a huge expanse of ocean. This previously put naval forces out of reach of many land-based or coastal weapon

Opposite: The *Visby* class corvette is a Swedish design intended to create a 'stealth ship' by greatly reducing thermal and radar signature compared to a conventional vessel of the same size.

systems, and made them hard to find even for those that had the range. Concealment is of paramount importance when operating within reach of a potential enemy.

Not coincidentally, 'stealth ships' have begun to emerge. These use advanced materials and shapes designed to reduce radar reflections in much the same manner that aircraft do. The Swedish *Visby* class corvette is perhaps the most notable of these vessels. A reduction in radar cross-section is of little use if the craft can be detected visually, so stealthy vessels tend to be small, with a low silhouette, and employ camouflage colouring.

None of these measures would be any real use if the craft gave away its location by other means such as radar emissions. As with active sonar, active radar pulses can be detected at much greater distances than they can detect other vessels. In recent years, a range of

LPI (low probability of intercept) radar and communications systems have been developed, although it will never be possible to completely eliminate the giveaway emissions of radar and radio systems.

Several nations have begun fielding forces of small missile-armed fast attack craft to defend their coastline. These vessels are not all 'stealth ships', but they tend to be small and thus difficult to detect using electronic sensors against the cluttered backdrop of a coastline. Well camouflaged or even hidden in concealed bunkers along the coast, these vessels may be able to gain the element of surprise against an enemy that comes inshore. This in turn contributes to both survivability and effectiveness: the less time an enemy has to react, the smaller his chance of evading or

Below: The six *Formidable* class frigates of the Republic of Singapore Navy were derived from a French design. They are 'stealth ships', designed with rapid transfer of information in mind. This means that platforms such as ships and aircraft can share sensor data, generating a clearer and detailed picture of the combat environment.

shooting down missiles launched by these coast defence boats.

There are several ways of defending against a missile attack. The most effective is to 'break the kill chain' by eliminating the attacking vessels before they can fire their weapons. Failing that, it is possible to shoot down the incoming weapons with missiles or rapid-fire guns or to use decoy systems. Decoys generally work by either distraction (confusing the missile guidance system by presenting additional possible targets) or seduction (presenting the weapon with a more attractive target).

Both measures are more effective if the missile is having a hard time finding or tracking its stealthy target. Similarly, the option of blanketing the whole target area with hot, radar-opaque smoke that prevents any form of sensor seeing the target works much better if the target has a small signature.

Coastal engagements are likely in any future conflict, and camouflage – of both traditional optical and more advanced electronic sorts – will continue to play an important part. Just as dazzle paintwork can confuse human gunners, the electronic equivalent confuses missiles and radar. 'Stealth' technologies that reduce the vessel's signature or return when detected by electronic sensors serve the same purpose as camouflage that hid vessels of previous eras from view. Nothing has really changed in principle; there are simply more kinds of eyes and ears now – and more ways to deceive them.

Right: *Sea Shadow* **was built in great secrecy as an experimental craft, implementing stealth technology and crew-reduction automation measures. It is indicative of how fast stealth technology has developed that** *Sea Shadow* **was highly secret until 1993, but in 2006 it was offered for sale on the open market – and no buyer came forward.**

THE FUTURE OF CAMOUFLAGE

The science of camouflage has undergone enormous development in the past few decades, but there are those who believe it has been finally outpaced by technological advance.

It is easy to believe that, in our modern world of advanced electronic sensors, camouflage in the traditional sense has no real future. This is not so; for every new sensor there is a countermeasure that can partially or completely blind it. Some of these countermeasures can be considered to be camouflage, and some are entirely different. However, both serve the same purpose – reducing the effectiveness of electronic sensor systems. Once advanced electronics are out of the picture, or are reduced in effectiveness, then traditional optical detection methods must be used.

There are many situations in which the opposition will not have access to sophisticated sensors. Terrorists and insurgent groups are unlikely to have much access to these systems, although occasionally an example of an advanced system will fall into their hands. The day when the average infantryman is tied into a complex sensor net at all times may come – maybe very soon – but even then he will rely on his eyes to confirm what his sensors are telling him.

Traditional optical camouflage thus remains a viable – even essential – part of the military arsenal. Now, as ever, a momentary confusion about what a soldier is seeing can make him miss a shot or fail to take cover in time. Images picked up by cameras of various sorts must still be interpreted by humans, and they can be fooled through a video screen just as readily as they can in person. By way of example, a battlefield view from a camera-equipped drone might be very useful, but it is not infallible. Camouflaged people and objects are far less readily identified than those that have dispensed with such antiquated methods.

Opposite: A US Navy SEAL in winter camouflage. Loose strips of cloth soften the outline of the soldier's body and his weapon. Even in today's highly technological world we still rely on the human eye for information, and the eye can still be fooled even through a video screen.

Above: A US Marine undergoes sniper training. He has used local flora to augment his ghillie suit to merge his shape with the local environment.

Indeed, in many situations camouflage may be more important than ever due to the environment in which most conflicts take place. With strict rules of engagement in place about what can and what cannot be fired upon, camouflage might be used to create just enough doubt that the opposition hesitates to attack. This is less likely to be the case in an all-out war, but in the modern world, 'war-like situations' with many rules and prohibitions in place are far more common than simple 'gentleman's wars'. Camouflage thus still has its uses, and the science of concealment continues to develop.

Infantry Camouflage Today

Traditionally, camouflage patterns have been based on natural shapes with irregular, 'soft'

edges. A system that uses any sort of straight line seems counterintuitive, as these do not occur in nature. However, digital camouflage began to emerge in the 1990s (earlier if Soviet 'stair step' designs are considered) and has been a success.

The term 'digital' camouflage can apply to any design created by a computer, although it is often used in a different context. Computer-designed camouflage makes use of highly complex algorithms that attempt to create the most effective concealment by the use of micropatterns. Rather than attempting to blend in with other natural shapes, digital camouflage instead relies on tricking the eye into not seeing what is there.

Digital camouflage might better be referred to as 'pixellated', since it makes use of precise pixels rather than general blobs of different colours. The terms are often used interchangeably, however. To date, all

camouflage of this nature uses micropatterns of pixels forming a macropattern that may be not dissimilar to a pixellated version of standard shapes used in conventional camouflage.

Some digital camouflage uses black lines along the edge of pixellated shapes, which creates the illusion of shadows. This causes the eye to try to interpret the camouflage as a number of three-dimensional shapes, thereby disguising the outline of whoever is wearing it. In order to work effectively, camouflage must not only conceal the outlines of distinctive parts of the body – such as the joints and the torso – but must also avoid repetition. The human eye is designed to pick out patterns, and a repetitive camouflage design can actually draw the eye by having the same shape repeated elsewhere on the body.

The key to creating effective digital camouflage is, according to some experts, to use fractal patterns. These repeat at any scale,

Above: The Chinese Type 07 'universal' pattern pixelated camouflage also comes in a blue 'ocean' version for marines and naval personnel.

thus depriving the eye of a frame of reference. This makes objects very difficult to discern. Pixellated camouflage thus works on the same basic principle as many other kinds – it does not so much prevent the eye from *seeing* an object as confuses the brain into not *recognizing* it.

However, pixellated camouflage is effective over a greater variety of ranges than conventional camouflage, which is typically restricted by the size of the shapes it uses. Where the size of the shapes on a camouflage pattern more or less matches the natural shapes around it as perceived by the eye, it tends to disappear into the background providing its colouration is reasonably close to that of the backdrop. At other ranges, the shapes on camouflage are larger or smaller than those surrounding it, and tend to be picked out by the eye as 'something different' that attracts a closer look. Some camouflage patterns are all but invisible at the right range but extremely obvious to an observer at a different distance.

PRECURSORS TO PIXELLATED CAMOUFLAGE

The principles underlying pixellated camouflage are not new. Very early camoufleurs used patterns of dots to create their designs, some of which were extremely effective. World War II-era *Erbsenmuster* (pea dot pattern) camouflage can be considered an ancestor of modern pixellated systems, and Soviet stair-step designs were also influential.

Pixellated camouflage is based on the principle that two things need to happen before the brain can make use of information from the eyes. First, it has to recognize that something is there, then a separate process has to resolve it into something recognizable. Most forms of camouflage attack one or other of these processes, but a pixellated system should

Deceiving the Eye

The concept of pixellated camouflage can seem strange – patterns of little squares do not exist in nature. However, it is not a question of what does or does not exist, but of what the eye perceives. Pixellated patterns deceive the human eye by denying it a frame of reference by which to gauge size. In addition, the definition of the pattern is lost to the eye at any distance greater than a few metres. The limitations of human vision soften the pattern and create the illusion of a smoothly blended shifting of colours and shapes.

be able to counter both. The micropatterns of the scheme confuse the eye into failing to note the presence of 'something different' to the background, while the macropatterns of the scheme make it difficult to resolve and recognize.

Right: A camouflage mask has the advantage that it can be used many times and can be put on or removed when needed.

Pixellated patterns typically use squares because these are relatively easy to produce on a computer. Other shapes could be used just as effectively, but present greater difficulties without offering any real advantages. It is important that the shapes used have clearly defined edges to allow patterns to be built very precisely, and that the pixels must be too small for the eye to resolve properly. That way, the patterns are seen rather than the blocks that form them. The end result is the creation of camouflage that mimics the colour and texture of the background as resolved by the human eye without specifically trying to copy it.

Creating an effective digital or pixellated camouflage design is thus anything but simple. It is possible to create effective traditional camouflage patterns by eye, but the creation of a pixellated scheme requires advanced mathematical algorithms. The relationship between colour layout of the pattern, and how the small patterns build larger ones, is extremely complex. A slight error can produce 'camouflage' that is counterproductive, and without a rigorous application of the science underlying camouflage it may not be possible to tell why this is or how far the pattern needs to be modified to become effective.

Pixellated camouflage is seen as desirable in some quarters for similar reasons to the adoption of Prussian-style uniforms in many nations after the Franco–Prussian war. This faulty line of thinking is driven as much by fashion as effectiveness. If pixellated camouflage can be created that is more effective than standard designs then it may be worth the investment. However, in some cases the desire to copy how highly effective combat forces dress may have outweighed this consideration.

Whether the US Army was influenced by MARPAT for the right reasons or the wrong

Above: Modern variants of the traditional camouflage paint are fairly quick to apply and remove. Some means of altering the distinctive appearance of the face will always be necessary, and paint or cream remains a simple and efficient way of doing so.

ones, its universal camouflage pattern (UCP), adopted in 2004, stands as an example of a failed pixellated design. Conceived, as the name suggests, as a solution to camouflage requirements in all environments. UCP cost around five billion dollars to create and implement, yet was found to be flawed in tests before it was issued. Nevertheless, UCP went into service for a time until MultiCam became available to replace it.

Testing and experimentation continues, and it may be that pixellated camouflage is the way forward. However, traditional schemes have been found in some tests to be more effective in certain conditions. All that is certain is that the science of camouflage is by no means fully developed, and that new ideas are not necessarily better than existing ones.

Above: Six different camouflage uniforms under testing at Fort Bliss in 2012. This exercise was to evaluate the degree of thermal reflection, and thus visibility to infrared devices, of each uniform under day and night conditions.

'Smart Camo' and Thermal Disguise

Advances in materials science have made it possible to create clothing that changes its colouration, which has obvious applications to camouflage. When colour change is a novelty, it does not really matter how precise it is nor how long it takes, but a camouflage system that can alter its colouring must obviously match the background very well. Such 'smart camo' is now a possibility, though at the time the developer began to demonstrate it something rather more exotic was already becoming available in the form of Quantum Stealth, a system that can completely conceal an object or person from observation. Little information is available on this system at the time of writing – its mechanism is a closely guarded secret.

The idea of a 'cloak of invisibility' can be found in fiction dating back hundreds of years, even to the legends of ancient religions. More recently 'cloaking devices' and similar near-magical stealth technologies have appeared in science-fiction and distinctly far-fetched drama. Conventional wisdom suggests that such a device makes an interesting story but cannot possibly be a reality. However, modern technology makes such a device a possibility.

It is possible to create a sort of 'invisibility device' by using cameras and displays, projecting an image of what is behind the object on its surface. If corrected for the shape of the object – not a simple matter – then such an image can create the illusion that the object is transparent. This can be used to hide something in the open where there is no cover, at least from visual detection.

Opposite: The ADAPTIV camouflage system, as shown on this tank, is a new technology designed to counter the proliferation of thermal imaging devices in the modern battlespace. It monitors the surrounding temperature conditions and heats or cools its elements to create the thermal image of some innocuous object or vehicle.

ADAPTIV

ADAPTIV, from BAE Systems, is a modular display system composed of hexagonal elements that can be cooled or heated to create a thermal image. ADAPTIV can be applied to helicopters, vehicles, ships and installations, with different sized elements being used to change the pixel size. Mimicking or hiding a building does not need the same fine level of control as concealing an armoured vehicle, but otherwise the method is much the same.

Using this device, it is possible to make an armoured vehicle appear, to thermal sensors, to be a car or even a cow. It can also be used to display recognition patterns. Individual elements can be swapped out if they become damaged, and control is also at the single-element level. This enables a considerable level of detail in the display; by using a database of known thermal signatures, the system can quite closely mimic specific types of vehicle or other disguises. The ADAPTIV system can also be used to display other kinds of image, including text.

While is it unlikely the military will ever receive a sponsorship deal to use its tanks as advertising billboards, the ADAPTIV system can be used to provide information or guidance in a humanitarian aid situation or to convey a non-threatening posture to those sighting vehicles equipped with it.

Above: This helicopter is covered in ADAPTIV hexagonal panels. The ADAPTIV system has a library of images it can display, though for a helicopter the best option is to match the surrounding thermal conditions.

However, to be useful as more than a curiosity, an 'invisibility device' must not only make an object visually undetectable but must also eliminate or alter its infra-red signature. Indeed, this capability is probably more important than optical invisibility, since thermal detection is one of the greatest threats faced in the modern battlespace.

Thermal detection and tracking systems are highly common and are available to even quite low-tech combatants due to advances in electronics. Finally, an 'invisibility device' must be sufficiently adaptive that it can be used on the move, and must not require prohibitively heavy, expensive or complex equipment.

Counters and Alternatives to Stealth

Low-observable ('stealth') technologies are expensive to develop and produce, and often require considerable effort to maintain in an operational environment. This is worth the effort in some circumstances, but for those who cannot afford technological stealth, or where effective countermeasures are in place, there are alternatives.

The use of terrain for concealment has never fundamentally changed, although the situation has become more complex. An aircraft or vehicle can still be lost in the background clutter if it positions itself between the detecting station and a suitable terrain feature such as a large hill. This primarily works against optical systems; advanced instruments can easily see a tank that is lost to the eye against the backdrop.

However, the technique is still useful. Low-flying helicopters or small boats can approach a ship from the landward side with a much smaller chance of detection and successful engagement, and a ship in littoral waters can be 'lost' against the shoreline to an observer out at sea. The trees of that shoreline can conceal artillery or rocket systems set up to attack vessels moving through a strait or operating close inshore.

Better concealment is offered by hiding behind something. Improved radar can detect low-flying aircraft from above much more readily than in the past, but to date there is no sensor system that can spot a target through a hill or large building. Thus, techniques like extreme low flying still allow aircraft to evade detection and cruise missiles to slip past defences. The world's most advanced air forces still train to fly up river valleys at very low level and to use a combination of low flight and high speed to minimize enemy engagement times. In this, little has changed, and concealment of this sort will remain useful to forces at all levels of sophistication for the foreseeable future.

There have been those who mistook 'stealth' technology for some sort of magical invisibility cloak, rendering its users invulnerable to radar and other sensors. In reality, every measure has its countermeasure and stealth of any kind has a limited lifespan of high effectiveness. After this it remains useful, especially against those who cannot afford to develop or purchase countermeasures, but it may be foolish to rely too much on any given technological solution.

Below: Low flying has always been an effective means of concealment for helicopters. There is a trade-off, however, between reduced observability at low altitude and vulnerability to small-arms fire from the ground.

Stealth Technologies and Radar

Most 'stealth' technologies are designed to reduce a particular component of an object's signature, such as its radar return. Indeed, some low-observable modifications are aimed at one particular wavelength of radar, such as that used by long-range air defence systems, and are not as effective against others. Radar that operates on more than one wavelength, combined with processing equipment that compares the return, can in some cases detect stealthy aircraft that would not be picked up by standard systems.

Bistatic and multistatic radar can also defeat some stealth technologies. Monostatic radar has the transmitter and receiver in the same place – the pulse goes out and comes straight back. If it is scattered and weakened, it may not be powerful enough to be picked up, but some stealth designs do not scatter radar energy as much as reflect it in a different direction. This creates a powerful return pulse but one that is directed somewhere else than the receiver – unless the target is unlucky enough to be caught at exactly the wrong angle. This setup is convenient, since

Bistatic radar

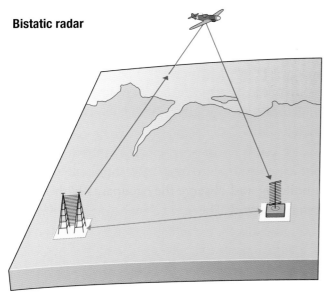

Multistatic radar

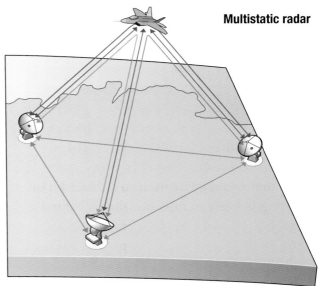

Above: A bistatic radar system can defeat some stealth designs, but relies on a reflection of radar energy in one direction. A multistatic system increases the chances of this occurring by having multiple transmitters.

it requires only one installation or location for a mobile radar set.

However, a bistatic or multistatic system has its receiver (or receivers) in different positions – possibly several positions. The receiver might be much closer to the transmitter than the target, and thus able to pick up weakened, scattered returns. It might also be positioned such that a reflected pulse strikes it despite being directed away from the receiver. Since stealth aircraft often attempt to slip through air defences by keeping the maximum distance between the flight path and the radar transmitters, this pact can take the aircraft right over the top of a receiver and generate a strong return.

It has even been suggested that a possible counter to stealth incursions is to use normal radio, television and mobile telephone broadcasts. These will be reflected, albeit weakly, by any aircraft passing overhead. A network of receivers could pick up these returns and feed them into a central processing and tracking system.

Combination sensors also offer real possibilities. An aircraft that is very difficult to detect using radar might have a stronger thermal signature, or vice versa. It might be that neither signature is strong enough to detect and track the aircraft, but by combining the two a clear position can be determined. The same applies to stealth versions of ships, armoured vehicles and the like – stealth can be countered and thus cannot be relied upon to protect the target. It is a highly useful capability, but not a magically all-powerful one.

Preventing Detection

Most stealth technologies attempt to prevent detection as well as concealing the target from those looking for it. This uses the same measures for the most part – if a bomber can be concealed from search radar then air defence tracking radars will never attempt to lock onto it, but even if detected its stealthy nature makes the bomber a difficult target to track. However, some measures make it more likely or even inevitable that the enemy will realize that *something* is there, but still conceal the target from any response that is made.

The use of a smokescreen type of camouflage makes it virtually certain that the enemy will notice the screen, and naturally infer that it is being made by a target. However, if the screen is larger than the target it obscures, it deprives the enemy of accurate targeting information. A missile that could guide itself to a direct hit on a warship is likely to miss one that is behind or inside a smokescreen larger than itself – although only if the screen is opaque to all of the missile's sensors.

This is the principle behind defensive systems such as MASS (Multi-Ammunition Softkill System). Upon detecting the emissions of enemy sensors, or when commanded to do so, MASS very rapidly deploys a smokescreen composed of materials that are opaque to radar and thermal sensors as well as visual ones. This can defeat self-guiding weapons such as most missiles, but is also effective against laser-guided weapons (as the laser cannot penetrate the smokescreen) and manually controlled optically guided weapons since these require the operator to see the target. An accidental hit is possible, but unlikely.

Right: The MASS system protects against guided weapons by hiding the target behind a fast-developing smokescreen that is opaque to radar and thermal sensors.

Another option, although one available only to certain weapon systems, is to be very small. Size plays an important part in detectability whatever other technologies might be in use. Unmanned air vehicles can be much smaller than a piloted aircraft, reducing their chances of being spotted, and some take this to an extreme. Micro-drones have an extremely limited range but are so small and quiet that they can enter a building and observe the occupants without being detected. There is no real chance of camouflaging a micro-drone or disguising it as something else; either it is spotted or it is not.

Above: The Black Hornet micro-drone is quiet enough to fly into a building suspected of being occupied by hostiles without alerting them. It has an endurance of 20 minutes, enabling personnel to see what is on 'the other side of the hill' without exposing them to risk.

However, its small size makes it unlikely to draw attention to itself.

Often, once a target is detected using electronic means it must then be identified, and this may require visual contact. Camouflage in the traditional sense, or systems that obscure the target, can provide an effective defence. However, all of this presupposes that the target can be identified as such. One alternative to

concealment – which has existed throughout human history – is to pretend to be inoffensive or non-hostile, i.e. to hide in plain sight.

Hiding in Plain Sight

Today's conflicts are increasingly asymmetric; they pit a technologically advanced and militarily highly capable force against one that cannot come close to matching its capabilities. This might seem like a recipe for defeat, yet it is not uncommon for a low-tech guerrilla or insurgent force to tie up the military of an advanced nation long enough to force it to the negotiating table. Camouflage in the traditional sense plays an essential role in such a conflict.

By remaining undetected, insurgents can stage an ambush or plant a roadside bomb, levelling the playing field to some extent. Well-equipped and supported regular forces still have an advantage in a close-range firefight, but not an overwhelming one.

There is, however, far more than this to the use of camouflage and deception in asymmetric warfare. One of the advantages enjoyed by insurgents is the fact that their opponents are typically bound by strict rules of engagement. If a target cannot be positively identified as hostile, often it cannot be engaged at all.

This can lead to blatant exploitation of the rules, such as the situation where an insurgent who has thrown a grenade may not be fired

Below: As technology advances, new opportunities arise for intelligence gathering. These aircraft are equipped for MASINT (Measurement and Signature Intelligence), using sensors to obtain data on the key signatures of the target. These can include radio, radar, infrared, chemical, nuclear and acoustic emissions, depending on the circumstances.

upon if all he does is flee. The insurgent can approach the target pretending to be an innocent person going about his business, and hang around waiting for a good opportunity. He is only in danger during the short moment between producing his weapon and making the attack.

Once his grenade is thrown or he has flung down his rifle, he is protected by rules of engagement. He can be pursued and apprehended, but cannot be fired upon – and if his attack is well planned then it may not be feasible to make any attempt at capture.

This is not always the case, but this situation has permitted insurgents to make blatant attacks on troops who were powerless to prevent it – and to get away with it. Traditional camouflage could be used before or after the attack to provide concealment, but in many cases it is more useful to hide in plain sight.

Hiding in plain sight, in this context, means appearing to be some innocent (or at least, not obviously hostile) person doing something insufficiently suspicious as to provoke a robust

Left: Drones and other remote camera platforms can gather data, but a camouflaged sniper, like this US special forces soldier, may still not be spotted.

response. How blatant the insurgent can be depends on the rules of engagement in force, and on the temperament of the troops involved. It is always possible that a response will be made whatever the rules may say, but this creates other issues.

In order to make an attack of this sort, the insurgents need to resemble someone who is not eligible to be fired upon. This might be an ordinary motorist, a group of local tribespeople, people going to work, or even rather suspicious individuals who are not obviously armed. Camouflage, in this case, is provided by an ordinary-seeming vehicle and/or clothing that matches what everyone else is wearing.

Weapons must be concealed or camouflaged, not least since many sets of rules of engagement are based around visible weapons or immediately credible threats. In cases where the weapon is a car bomb or suicide vest, it can be extremely difficult to tell the suicide bomber from any other person by appearance alone; behaviour provides the only clues. If weapons such as firearms are to be used they must be concealed until deployed, or camouflaged in some way. It can be difficult to disguise a rifle or machine gun as something innocent, so more commonly weapons are concealed until needed.

Hiding in plain sight in this manner is useful when undertaking all manner of activities. It would be extremely difficult to move supplies, ammunition or weapons around in the face of a technologically superior opponent without concealing them in some manner. Sneaking along concealed routes has been effective at times – for example, the Ho Chi Minh Trail during the Vietnam War. However, in the modern environment it is often easier to move equipment and personnel in plain sight.

This requires blending in with innocent vehicular traffic and not attracting attention. Even if there are checkpoints to negotiate, if the insurgents do not arouse suspicion then they may be able to proceed quite freely. There is only so much that can be done with the manpower available without bringing normal life to a standstill, which is something that most technologically advanced powers do not have the option of doing. Indeed, a security lockdown that catches arms shipments but angers the local populace may do the insurgents' cause more good than the weapons would have done.

Similarly, if insurgents can create a situation where innocents are fired upon, this can greatly

aid their cause. If the 'actual bad guys' act a lot like innocent people, then the actions of many innocents – especially those who resent the presence of a foreign military and are less than cooperative – may seem suspicious. A completely innocent but angry person who has lost patience with the checkpoint system (or the treatment he has received at checkpoints) and who decides not to stop may become an inadvertent martyr to the insurgents' cause. This in turn can stir up additional ill feeling or may influence the attitudes of the voting public. The outcome of many modern conflicts is decided as much in the living rooms of television viewers as they are fought in the fields and on the streets. News of an innocent shot dead for not stopping at a military checkpoint can inspire anti-war feeling, which in turn can lead to pressure from voters to pull out of the conflict zone. Most insurgents do not really care why the troops were withdrawn

Below: Despite repeated US efforts to close it, the Ho Chi Minh Trail was used to transport ammunition and supplies to insurgents fighting in South Vietnam.

Above: Improvised Explosive Devices (IEDs) are increasingly in use by insurgents worldwide. To be effective, most IEDs have to be concealed or camouflaged in some manner, blending into the local scene.

so long as they were. It really does not matter whether a foreign power was defeated in the field or its deployment made too expensive. Nor is it important whether the decision to withdraw was based on strategy or a need to avoid defeat in the next election. All that matters to the insurgents is that they have won.

Incidents in the Field

Examples of the complicated situation faced by military personnel include the USS *Cole* incident, the USS *Stark* incident and the Iranian Airbus incident. In May 1987, USS *Stark* was on patrol in the Persian Gulf when it detected an unidentified aircraft. This aircraft, which turned out to be an Iraqi Mirage F1 armed with Exocet missiles, did

not respond to attempts to contact it, but was not fired upon. The Iraqi jet fired two missiles at USS *Stark*, failing to sink it but inflicting serious damage and considerable loss of life.

A little over a year later, in July 1988, USS *Vincennes*, also on patrol in the Persian Gulf, detected an unknown aircraft that might have been on an attack run. The aircraft did not respond to attempts to contact it and was fired upon by *Vincennes*, which had recently been engaged in surface action against Iranian gunboats. In accordance with the current rules of engagement, USS *Vincennes* fired missiles and downed the aircraft, which was later identified as a civilian airliner.

US and Iranian versions of events differ considerably, and it has even been suggested that the incident was deliberate on the part of the Iranian authorities. This would be very difficult to prove either way, but these incidents serve to illustrate the problems faced by military forces in

Above: The attack on USS *Cole* exploited rules of engagement which have since been changed. There still remains the possibility of attackers hiding in plain sight by pretending to be innocents, or at least creating sufficient doubt about their intentions that defenders cannot open fire in time to prevent the attack.

came alongside just after *Cole* finished fuelling in Aden harbour. The explosives were detonated, seriously damaging USS *Cole* and causing numerous fatalities among its crew.

Even after this attack, gunners who trained their weapons on a second boat that was acting suspiciously were ordered to move their aim elsewhere as it had demonstrated no hostile intent. What sort of warning might have been available before a second suicidal detonation is a matter for speculation. It is notable that rules of engagement have evolved since this incident, but the problem of telling innocents from hostiles hiding among them remains a thorny one.

Blending In

This situation can be exploited in various ways. The most obvious is to attack by surprise of course, but it is also possible to further the cause of an insurgency or terrorist movement by what amounts to a double bluff. By making attacks – successful or otherwise – after hiding among innocents, it may be possible for insurgents to provoke an excessive response (or one that can be presented as excessive). For example, repeated threats and provocations might be used to escalate tension in the hope that a nervous embassy guard or security patrol might open fire on an innocent.

This can be taken further, if the insurgency contains people willing to accept the risks. After a period of escalated tension and incidents designed to test the patience and restraint of guards, an insurgent might deliberately make an action

such an environment. The USA was not at war with Iran or Iraq at the time of these incidents, although they were at war with one another.

US warships were deployed in a very dangerous area of the world in order to protect civilian shipping, which had come under attack despite being wholly uninvolved in the conflict. Short of withdrawing all shipping from one of the world's most important waterways, there was really no alternative to deploying naval forces, but this in turn exposed them to attack. The ambiguity of the situation could lead to ships being attacked without sufficient warning to defend themselves, or mistakenly firing upon perceived threats and taking innocent lives.

The United States was not at war in October 2000 when USS *Cole* was attacked in a supposedly friendly harbour. A small boat packed with explosives and crewed by two men that will be perceived as an imminent threat. Afterward, it will be seen that there was no gun, no bomb, and no real threat, but by that time the incident will be causing controversy worldwide.

The question of how to prevent such an occurrence without resorting to a trigger-happy mentality has been discussed for many years. Unless a technological solution presents itself, such as biometric recognition of known insurgents or terrorists, the only guide to intentions is behaviour. Some actions are unmistakably hostile, although even then there is the possibility of a deliberate provocation.

As a rule, however, behaviour can be seen as the key to an informed decision about what

Below: In March 2016, suicide bombers attacked targets in Belgium. This man is thought to be one of the perpetrators. The difficulty inherent in telling a terrorist or insurgent from any other person with luggage is obvious.

response is appropriate. Experienced law enforcement and security personnel can often tell that someone is somehow 'off' just by glancing at them. Often they cannot say exactly what the 'tells' are, just that the person is not behaving the way an innocent person would. This is not perfect; some assassins have been able to suppress their natural tension and nervousness to the point where they do not arouse suspicion, for example.

Most people cannot come close to this degree of self-control, of course. This is especially true of someone about to launch a suicide bomber attack or to open fire on military personnel he has been conditioned to hate. There are often personal indications that the individual is about to do something violent, but these can only serve as a warning if he is observed. One way to avoid that is to strike from concealment; another is deception.

Conclusions

The science of camouflage is constantly developing, with new technologies emerging that can seem like something drawn from science fiction. Despite this, nothing has really changed. The purpose of camouflage and all related measures remains the same – to avoid detection and to make identification and targeting difficult for the enemy.

This can be achieved by pretending to be something harmless (mimesis) or by being difficult to see (crypsis). It can also be achieved by complex technical methods that confuse the eye or defeat advanced sensors, or by creating sufficient doubt in the mind of the observer that he hesitates to shoot. Paired with decoys and dummies, camouflage continues to contribute to the ambiguity of the battle situation. Clear and useful information has always been a vital part of warfare, and there are more ways than ever to deny it to the enemy.

THE FUTURE OF CAMOUFLAGE

Concealment Through Desensitization

It is possible to conceal intentions by desensitizing the prospective target to certain actions. The 'two guys on a jetski' scenario serves as an example. Warships in port maintain a secure area around them, and personnel are usually permitted to make a robust response to those who enter the secure area and ignore warnings. However, it is more difficult to deal with encroachment at water level.

If jetskis are a common sight in the harbour, then one straying a bit too close to the ship might not arouse much suspicion. Over several days, these swimsuit-clad jetskiers repeatedly ignore warnings to move away, but never encroach sufficiently as to provoke a heavy-handed response. Eventually, the crew of a warship in port become used to having to warn jetskiers away several times before they finally obey. They have become desensitized to incursions.

Eventually, the insurgents make their attack. Amid the usual playful 'teasing' of the warship, a jetski comes too close and ignores warnings to turn away. This is not unduly alarming; it happens all the time. But on this occasion, the passenger is armed with an RPG-7. By the time it is noticed and a response made, it is too late. A rocket-propelled grenade will not sink a warship, but it will kill and injure crew members, cause damage and perhaps humiliate the powerful navy thus attacked. Voters may begin to ask why the navy is 'out there' taking casualties in peacetime.

This is just one of many possible scenarios that depend not upon camouflage of people or objects as such, but upon deception and concealment of intentions. The principle is the same, whether the attacker wears disruptive camouflage and uses a sniper rifle or dons a brightly coloured jacket and joins a band of noisy but harmless and entirely innocent protestors to get close to his target. The means may vary but the intent is always the same; to deceive the enemy and thereby to gain an advantage.

Some forms of camouflage are really quite unusual. There was, for a time, a plan to protect part of the US nuclear strike capability by concealing missiles aboard trains that would be inserted into normal rail traffic. Outwardly resembling a fairly typical goods train, the route of any given missile would be a closely guarded secret; at any given time it could be almost anywhere on the rail network. This created additional difficulty in targeting the weapon even if its location and route were known.

Other forms of 'camouflage-like activity' include barefaced denial of existence. Guards at the gate of certain structures will politely deny the existence of certain buildings, even ones that are visible over their shoulders. By refusing to release any information about a structure and not permitting anyone near it without authorization, the government can conceal what is going on inside. Indeed, there is no way to be sure such structures are not red herrings – it may be that a secret site is nothing but a decoy, and the activities 'everyone knows' are

Opposite: This US Navy SEAL's woodland camouflage offers good concealment as soon as he stops moving. Other methods of concealment may become prevalent but the benefits of traditional camouflage are well proven.

Above: Since the mid-1990s, the Kurdish people of Iraq have fielded small numbers of female *Peshmergas* (loosely translated as 'one who stands in front of death') and one regular all-female battalion. Their equipment varies considerably, with weapons and uniforms coming from a variety of sources. This woman wears a digital desert camouflage uniform of uncertain origin.

carried out there are actually based elsewhere. In the modern world, where private citizens have access to phones and drones equipped with cameras, and even to satellite imagery, hiding anything can seem like a very difficult undertaking. It is possible to blur out areas on satellite images – certain sites are blanked out of commercially available satellite maps – but this only works if the satellite operator is willing to cooperate. It is certainly no use against foreign reconnaissance satellites.

The only real answer is to apply the principles of deception and camouflage in new and inventive ways. Even if a building cannot be concealed, its purpose can be. Movements of critical personnel can be disguised by using several identical vehicles either together or proceeding separately. It is not uncommon for dignitaries to arrive at their destination before their officially posted itinerary says they will be leaving the start point, and sometimes the ostentatious motorcade is a decoy while the VIP travels in a plain vehicle or military transport.

There is a rule of thumb in the security industry that the more obvious someone's bodyguards and security personnel are, the less important they tend to be. Ostentatious 'minders' are a fashion accessory to demonstrate how rich and influential someone is, or perhaps to distract attention from other security personnel. High-end security is unobtrusive, with some of the protection team camouflaged as lawyers and other advisors, or hidden in the crowds dressed as ordinary people.

Even those who are overt tend not to be ostentatious – it is a reasonable assumption that the athletic young people in nice suits who surround a VIP

Right: The bodyguards around Russian premier Vladimir Putin are all dressed similarly to him. A would-be assassin would need to take extra time to be sure he is attacking the right target, possibly offering enough time to react or to escape.

might well be bodyguards, but it can be difficult to be sure. There is one other consideration here; if bodyguards wear suits of approximately the same colour as the person they are protecting, then they provide an element of protective colouration as they hustle their charge to safety. This is no different to the dazzle camouflage of a zebra – the target can be lost in the herd, or at least an assailant might be confused long enough to prevent a successful attack.

Thus, camouflage in the modern world can take the form of a military uniform designed by advanced computer systems, or it could be a brightly coloured jacket like all the other innocent tourists are wearing. It can be created with locally available materials or produced in an advanced materials laboratory. There are now more options than ever before.

Emerging technologies might offer entirely new capabilities in the future. All that is certain is that there are advantages to be gained from being hard to see and identify. That has not changed and it will not change in any foreseeable future. Thus, the art and science of camouflage will continue to develop, and it will continue to be applied in new and creative ways.

INDEX

Numbers in *italics* refer to illustrations

PICTURE CREDITS

Alamy: 12 (Scott Camazine), 13 (Michele Burgess), 15 (Interfoto), 17 (Chronicle), 24 (Annie Eagle), 37 (Rhyor Bruyeu),
    40 (SOTK2011), 53l (Military Images), 80 (Andrew Chittock), 83 (Agenja Fotograficzna Caro), 124 (Frank Tschope),
    129 (Kevin Frayer), 145 (Aviation One), 152 (Military Images), 164 (Chronicle), 170b (Granger Collection), 182 (War
    Archive), 190 (Wayne Farrell), 199 (Reuters)
Art-Tech: 28, 43, 94, 122, 126/127, 137, 139, 143, 176, 177, 185, 189, 212
BAE Systems: 162, 203, 204
Cody Images: 18, 34, 98, 102, 104, 111, 168, 174, 191
Depositphotos: 87 (Bloodua)
Dreamstime: 62 (Gary Blakeley), 74l (Wirojsid), 75 (Libo Tang)
Getty Images: 11 (De Agostini), 19 (AFP/Patrick Baz), 27 (Hulton), 35 (Universal Images Group), 36 (Hulton),
    38 (Popperfoto), 42 (Archive Photos), 61 (Life), 65 (Bettmann), 67 (Corbis), 69 (AFP), 74r (Hulton), 77 (Paris Match
    Archive/Bruno Bachelet), 92 (Corbis), 99 (IWM), 112 (Life), 115 (Archive Photos), 130 (Scott Nelson), 140 (Hulton),
    141 (Hulton), 156 (Hulton), 157 (IWM), 165 (Popperfoto), 167 (Hulton), 170t (SSPL), 178 (Time Life), 215 (Anadolu
    Agency), 218 (Light Rocket), 219 (Gamma-Rapho/Konstantin Zavrazhin)
Kockums: 192
Library of Congress: 10, 97t
Mediatus: 45c (CC by SA 3.0)
Obrum: 131
Bertil Olofsson/Krigsarkivet: 32, 96
Prox Dynamics: 208
Rheinmetal: 207
Ukrainian State Archive: 56, 57, 107, 117
U.S. Department of Defense: 6, 8, 9, 14 both, 16, 21, 22, 58, 78, 81, 84, 85, 86, 88, 93, 97b, 120, 121, 123, 132, 159–161
    all, 186–188 all, 193, 195, 198, 200–202, 205, 209, 210, 213, 214, 217
U.S. Marine Corps Art Collection: 50
U.S. Navy SEALs: 90, 196

All artworks © Art-Tech, except page 108 © Oliver Missing (www.o5m6.de/)